■ □ ■ □ ■

LIGHTNING FROM THE DEPTHS

■ □ ■ □ ■

LIGHTNING
FROM THE DEPTHS

AN ANTHOLOGY OF
ALBANIAN POETRY

Edited and translated from the Albanian
by Robert Elsie and Janice Mathie-Heck

NORTHWESTERN UNIVERSITY PRESS

EVANSTON, ILLINOIS

Northwestern University Press
www.nupress.northwestern.edu

Printed in the United States of America

10 9 8 7 6 5 4 3 2 1

Library of Congress Cataloging-in-Publication Data

Lightning from the depths : an anthology of Albanian poetry / edited and translated
from the Albanian by Robert Elsie and Janice Mathie-Heck.
    p. cm.—(Writings from an unbound Europe)
Includes bibliographical references.
ISBN-13: 978-0-8101-2462-2 (cloth : alk. paper)
ISBN-10: 0-8101-2462-9 (cloth : alk. paper)
ISBN-13: 978-0-8101-2463-9 (pbk. : alk. paper)
ISBN-10: 0-8101-2463-7 (pbk. : alk. paper)
    1. Albanian poetry—Translations into English. I. Elsie, Robert, 1950– II. Mathie-
Heck, Janice, 1950–
PG9665.E54L55 2008
891'.9911008—dc22

                                                                2008013793

■ □ ■ □ ■

CONTENTS

POETRY IN THE MUSLIM TRADITION

ITALO-ALBANIAN VERSE

RILINDJA AND CLASSICAL
TWENTIETH-CENTURY POETRY

■ □ ■ □ ■

INTRODUCTION

Geographically, Albania has always been at the crossroads of empires and civilizations, even though it has often been isolated from the mainstream of European history. For centuries in ancient times, it formed the political, military, and cultural border between East and West, that is, between the Roman Empire of the western Mediterranean, including much of the northern Balkans, and the Greek Empire of the eastern Mediterranean, including the southern Balkans. In the Middle Ages, Albania was once again a buffer zone, this time between Catholic Italy and the Byzantine Greek Empire. Later, after its definitive conquest by the Ottoman Empire in the fifteenth century, it formed a bridgehead between Christian Europe and the Islamic Orient. As a geographical and cultural entity, and as a nation, Albania has always been somewhat enigmatic and misunderstood. In the eighteenth century, historian Edward Gibbon (1737–94) described it as a land within sight of Italy and less known than the interior of America. The spirit of this quotation has lost surprisingly little of its validity over the last two centuries. Bordering Greece and what was once Yugoslavia, and less than one hundred kilometers from the southern Italian coast, Albania has until very recently been no better known to most other Europeans than Tibet or Timbuktu.

The Albanians are among the longest-established inhabitants of southeastern Europe, having lived in that rugged, mountainous terrain since ancient times. Their presence there has been documented for about a thousand years, but their roots go back much further. A great deal of speculation has been offered about their origins, in particular by the Albanians themselves, who are passionately interested in tracing their roots and in establishing their autochthony in the Balkans. Despite this, nothing has been proven conclusively. What we can say with reasonable certainty is that there is no evidence indicating that the Albanians immigrated to their present homeland in the southwest Balkans from anywhere else. As such, it may be safely assumed that they are indigenous to the region, as opposed to their Slavic neighbors, who invaded the Balkans from the north in the sixth and seventh centuries. In view of this autochthony, it can also be taken for granted that the Albanians are, in some form, descendants of the ancient peoples of the southern Balkans. To what extent they are the direct heirs of the Illyrians, the Dardanians, the Thracians, the Bessians, some lesser-known people, or a mixture thereof, is a matter that has been much discussed and to which substantial controversy has been attached from the earliest writings on the subject in the eighteenth century to the present. It is particularly difficult to fathom the genesis of a people from the Balkan Peninsula, a place that has baffled scholars from Herodotus to recent generations of history students trying to sort out the Balkan wars.

Unfortunately, we possess no original documents from the first millennium A.D. that could help us trace the Albanians further back into history. They were nomadic tribes in the interior of the peninsula that seem only rarely to have ventured down onto the marshy and mosquito-infected coastline. As such, they long went unnoticed, and their early history is thus shrouded in mist. An account of the Albanians must best depart from the moment they entered the annals of recorded history. The first references to them date from the eleventh century, a period in which these tribes were beginning to expand their settlements and consolidate as a people and as a nation. It is only in this age that we may speak with any degree of clarity about an Albanian people as we know them today. Their traditional designation, based on a root *alban- and its rhotacized variants *arban-, *albar-, and *arbar-, first appears in the eleventh century in Byzantine chronicles (Albanoi, Arbanitai, Arbanites), and later, in the fourteenth century, in Latin and other Western documents (Albanenses, Arbanenses).

With time, and with innate vigor, unconscious persistence, and much luck, they came to take their place among the nation-states of Europe. However, even in the twenty-first century, the phrase "nation-state of Europe" may seem inappropriate for the Albanians. Their life and their culture are those of a developing country, of a third-world nation struggling for survival in every sense of the word. In material terms, they have been deprived of all but the bare essentials needed to stay alive. Indeed, the historical, political, economic, and cultural development of the Albanians has been so arduous that those who know them well can do little but marvel at how they have managed to survive as a people at all.

The Albanian Language

The Albanian language, an Indo-European idiom spoken by about seven million people in the Balkans and in the diaspora, is divided into two basic dialect groups: Gheg in the north and Tosk in the south. The Shkumbin River in central Albania, flowing past Elbasan into the Adriatic, forms the approximate border between the two groups. The Gheg dialect group is characterized by the presence of nasal vowels, by the retention of the older *n* for Tosk *r* (for example, Gheg *venë* [wine] for Tosk *verë*, Gheg *Shqypnia* [Albania] for Tosk *Shqipëria*), and by several distinctive morphological features. The modern literary language (*gjuha letrare*), agreed upon, though not without political pressure, in 1972, is a combination of the two dialect groups but based to about 80 percent on Tosk. It is now a widely accepted standard in Albania, Kosova (Kosovo), and Macedonia, although there have been attempts recently to revive literary Gheg.

In addition to three million speakers in Albania itself, the Albanian language is also spoken by two to three million individuals in what was once Yugoslavia. The Albanian population is found primarily in Kosova, where it constitutes about 87 percent of the population; the remaining 13 percent are primarily BCS (Bosnian, Croatian, Serbian), Turkish, and Roma speakers. The mother tongue of most Kosovar Albanians is a northeastern Gheg dialect, though the majority of publications there, as in Albania, are in standard literary Albanian. In the southern Republic of Macedonia, Albanian speakers make up about a quarter of the total population. The Macedonian capital Skopje, which has one of the largest Albanian populations of any city on earth, serves as a secondary center for Albanian publishing and culture, though it is less important than Prishtina, which vies with Tirana in every way as a focal point of Albanian literary and cultural activity and as a publishing center for Albanian literature. A substantial minority of Albanian speakers (about 8 percent) is also found in the Republic of Montenegro, mostly along the Albanian border in the regions of Gucia/Gusinje and Plava/Plav in the mountains, Tuz/Tuzi south of Podgorica (formerly Titograd), and Ulqin/Ulcinj on the southern coast. There are, in addition, Albanian speakers throughout southern Serbia and indeed in virtually all other regions of the former Yugoslav federation, many of whom migrated from the economically destitute Kosovar region to the more affluent republics of the north (Croatia and Slovenia) in search of freedom, jobs, and a better standard of living.

A surprise to many is the existence of a traditional Albanian minority in southern Italy, the so-called Arbëresh. They are the descendants of refugees who fled Albania after the death of Skanderbeg (George Castrioti) in 1468. Due to a more favorable social and political environment than that in the Balkans, the Arbëresh were able to make a decisive contribution to the evolution of Albanian literature and to the nationalist movement in the nineteenth century. Older Albanian literature is indeed to a large extent Arbëresh literature. As a linguistic minority, the Arbëresh now consist of about twenty thousand active speakers, most of whom live in the mountain villages of Cosenza in Calabria and in the vicinity of Palermo in Sicily. Their language is moribund due to the strong cultural influence of Italian and to economic emigration. It is extremely archaic and differs substantially from the Albanian spoken in the Balkans. Communication is difficult if Arbëresh speakers are not familiar with standard literary Albanian.

In Greece, the sizable stratum of Albanians who populated much of central and southern Greece in the Middle Ages has been largely assimilated. The old Albanian language there, known in Greek as Arvanitika, can nonetheless still be heard in about 320 villages, primarily those of Boeotia (especially around Levádhia), southern Euboea, Attica, Corinth and the Peloponnese Peninsula, and northern Ándros. No official statistics exist as to the number of speakers since the language does not enjoy any official status. Arvanitika, which is dying out rapidly, is thought to be the most archaic form of Albanian spoken today. A large Albanian community still exists in Turkey (Istanbul, Bursa, and elsewhere). The ranks of these Ottoman Albanians were swelled by an estimated 230,000 Yugoslav Albanians who were expelled from their native land between 1953 and 1966 and forced to emigrate to Turkey. Finally, Albanian speakers in varying numbers are to be encountered among the migrant workers of Europe, in particular in Greece, Italy, Germany, and Switzerland, and also in the traditional countries of immigration, the United States (New York, Boston, Detroit) and Canada (Toronto), and to a lesser extent in Australia, New Zealand, and Argentina.

Albanian Literature

Compared to the other national languages of Europe, Albanian does not enjoy a long literary tradition. In fact, it was the last national language of Europe to establish a written tradition. Nor was the establishment of a literary culture in Albania ever an easy task, though not for want of artistic endeavor and creative impulses. All too often the tempestuous course of Albanian history has nipped the flowers of Albanian literature in the bud and severed the roots of intellectual culture.

However, poetry has been an integral part of the life of the Albanians for centuries. Even today, the poet is a highly respected figure in Albanian society, and rare is the intellectual who has not tried his or her hand at verse.

The earliest poetry written and recorded in Albanian dates from the sixteenth and seventeenth centuries and had a primarily religious focus. It was composed by authors who were raised in the traditions of the Catholic Church, for the most part not in Albania itself but in Italy. The earliest poem that we know of, written in 1592, is by an Italo-Albanian cleric from Sicily, Lekë Matrënga, who had probably never been to Albania at all. Other early authors, like Pjetër Budi and Pjetër Bogdani, who were from the Balkans though they published their works in Italy, wrote verse of primarily religious inspiration and had evident difficulty putting their rough, unpolished idiom to paper. The traditions of Albanian verse in Italy were later furthered by the Albanian minority living in the mountains of Calabria and Sicily.

In Albania itself, the early tradition of Catholic poetry might have provided a foundation for literary creativity in the age of the Counter-Reformation under the somewhat ambiguous patronage of the Catholic Church had not the banners of Islam soon been unfurled on the eastern horizon and tiny Albania been destined to bear the full brunt of the Turkish invasion in the late fourteenth century. Subsequently, the majority of the Albanian population converted to Islam. The Ottoman colonization of Albania, which had begun as early as 1385, split the country into three spheres of culture, all virtually independent of one another: (1) the cosmopolitan traditions of the Islamic Orient using initially Turkish, Persian, and Arabic as their media of literary expression and later employing Albanian in a stylized Aljamiado literature, the so-called poetry of the Bejtexhinj; (2) the lingering Byzantine heritage of Greek Orthodoxy in southern Albania, which produced a number of religious and scholarly works in Greek script in the eighteenth century; and (3) the awakening culture and literature of the Arbëresh in southern Italy, nourished by a more favorable social, political, and economic climate and by the fertile intellectual soil of Italian civilization.

A new poetic culture arose and flourished within the Muslim tradition. While the Ottoman Empire, with its centralist organization and power base focused in Istanbul, left Albania the cultural and political backwater it had been beforehand, Ottoman Turkish culture, which reached its zenith during the Tulip Age of the eighteenth century, penetrated the country thoroughly. Southern and central Albanian cities like Berat and Elbasan, with their newly constructed fortifications, mosques, and medresas, became provincial centers of Oriental learning and indeed experienced something of a cultural renaissance under Islam, as did the northern towns of Shkodra, Gjakova, and Prizren. Wandering poets, minstrels, and scholars enjoyed the patronage of local governors and pashas, as they did throughout Asia Minor. Nezim Frakulla and Hasan Zyko Kamberi are excellent examples of this tradition. Of all the periods of Albanian writing, however, the Muslim tradition remains the least known, both by specialists and by the Albanian reading public. Many manuscripts have not yet been transcribed, as there is a conspicuous dearth of experts qualified to deal with this literature on a scholarly basis.

The stable foundations of an Albanian national literature were finally laid in the second half of the nineteenth century with the rise of the nationalist movement for autonomy within a decaying Ottoman Empire. The literature of this so-called Rilindja ("Rebirth") period of national awakening was one of romantic nationalism and provides an excellent key to an understanding of the Albanian mentality. The Albanians were striving for the consolidation of their ethnic and cultural identity within the vast Ottoman Empire, and this set them on the course to aspire to independence. Poets such as Pashko Vasa and Naim Bey Frashëri stirred feelings of nationhood and ethnic assertiveness with their verse, works known and recited by Albanians even today. As so often in the history of Albanian literature, the very act of writing in Albanian constituted a gesture of defiance against the foreign powers ruling the country or dominating it culturally. Indeed, the Sublime Porte regarded most Albanian cultural and educational activity as subversive, and as such, saw fit to ban Albanian-language schools and the publication of all books and periodicals in Albanian. With no access to education in their own language, only a small minority of Albanians could hope to break through the barriers to intellectual thought and literary creativity.

At the beginning of the twentieth century, the Catholic education facilities set up by the Jesuits and Franciscans in Shkodra under the auspices of the Austro-Hungarian Kultusprotektorat paved the way for the creation of an intellectual elite in Albania, which in turn produced the rudiments of a more sophisticated literature that expressed itself primarily in verse.

Albania finally attained independence in 1912. The struggle for nation building had ended, and Albanian became the official language of the new country. The poets of the early twentieth century were now able to use their talents for purely aesthetic endeavors rather than as a vehicle for nationalist struggle. Independent Albania soon developed a solid literature with a broad range of pleasurable and interesting poets. Among them, in particular, was the talented

Franciscan pater Gjergj Fishta, lauded intermittently as the national poet of Albania, who, in 1937, finished the definitive version of his stirring national epic *The Highland Lute*.

Modern Albanian poetry can be said to date from the 1930s. It begins its course with two poets in particular: Migjeni and Lasgush Poradeci. Migjeni (acronym of Millosh Gjergj Nikolla), from Shkodra, who died of tuberculosis at the tender age of twenty-six, was one of the first poets to abandon the long-standing tradition of romantic nationalism in Albanian verse. His poetry, collected in the slender volume *Free Verse* (*Vargjet e lira*), is characterized by a strong social ethic, not of pity for the poor but of outrage against injustice and oppression. Lasgush Poradeci, from the town of Pogradec, on Lake Ohrid, on the other hand, who had very little in common with his contemporaries—the romantic Asdreni, the political Fan Noli, or the messianic Migjeni—imbued Albanian letters with an exotic element of pantheistic mysticism, introducing what he called the metaphysics of creative harmony. Although he remained an outsider, his stylistic finesse was decisive in enriching and diversifying Albanian poetic meters. Migjeni and Poradeci liberated Albanian verse from the traditions of the past and took it to unprecedented heights. This modest golden age, however, soon came to an abrupt end.

The flourishing literature of prewar Albania was swept away by the political revolution that took place in the country during and after World War II and was replaced by a radically proletarian and socialist literature. However, the heavy-handed application of the literary doctrine of socialist realism, introduced and made obligatory by 1949, and the intimidation and terror exerted upon writers and intellectuals by the new Stalinist regime created the opposite of what the doctrine intended—a cultural vacuum that lasted for more than two decades. The results of this oppressive period of fear and stagnation can still be felt today. Few works of sustaining aesthetic value were produced or published in Albania in this period, although a handful of writers—some of whom, like Martin Camaj, were in exile—managed to produce works of stunning beauty.

When the Communists came to power in 1944, under Enver Hoxha (1908–85), substantial efforts were nonetheless made for the first time to provide the broad masses of the population with basic education. The postwar mass literacy campaign constituted a revolution in itself and paved the way for a real national literature that could encompass all strata of society. In order to appreciate the reasons for the comparatively late blossoming of a written literature in Albania, one must keep in mind the fact that up to the 1950s, 80 percent of the population of the country, including virtually all the women, were illiterate. The twentieth century arrived late in Albania.

Despite the dictatorship, Albanian poetry managed to evolve. By the 1960s, writers had learned to wrap the requisite political messages and propaganda in innovative layers of aesthetics, endeavoring to appease the exasperation of the reading public. The foundations for this new literature were laid by a fresh generation of writers in search of something new, led by Fatos Arapi (1930–), Dritëro Agolli (1931–), and Ismail Kadare (1936–).

Works by Albanian authors in Kosova and Macedonia also began appearing in this period, and what they published, more than anything else, was lyric poetry. The extreme political divergence between Yugoslavia and Albania that erupted in 1948 made it evident to Kosovar Albanians from the start that they could not look to Tirana for more than moral support in culture and education. The preservation and fostering of Albanian culture in Yugoslavia under often hostile conditions were of necessity to be the concern of Yugoslav Albanians themselves. Similar to the situation in Albania, the formidable problems posed by widespread illiteracy and dire poverty among the Albanians in Kosova were substantially compounded by a persistent unwillingness on the part of the Serbian authorities in Belgrade to give the Albanians access to education and cultural facilities in their own language. After much delay, full cultural autonomy was first achieved under the constitution of 1974, but in 1990, Kosova lost its limited autonomy and freedom and was placed under direct Serbian military occupation. In 1999, the international community finally liberated Kosova from dictatorship after a decade of fear and oppression under the Milošević regime.

Though lacking the richer literary traditions of Serbian, Croatian, and Slovenian, the literature of the Kosovar Albanians evolved rapidly and is now just as dynamic as that of other parts of the Balkans. Unburdened by the ideological constraints imposed on literature and culture in Tirana during the Stalinist regime, the literature of Kosova was able to flourish free of dogma and maintain a certain defiance. Thus, with regard to the diversity and expressiveness of its poets, in some respects it surpassed that of Albania itself.

Whether written in Albania, Kosova, or elsewhere, Albanian literature is young and dynamic, reflecting a culture unique in Europe. But perhaps no European literature has been so neglected by Western readers, a neglect fostered by the lack of translations, of specialists in Albanian, and, in the second half of the twentieth century, by Albania's political isolation. If Edward Gibbon's remark about Albania is still valid, the real terra incognita is Albanian literature.

The tender plant of Albanian literature grew in a rocky soil. Time and again it sprouted and blossomed, and, time and again, it was torn out of the earth by the brutal course of political history in the Balkans. The early literature of Christian Albania disappeared under the banners of Islam when the country was forcefully incorporated into the Ottoman Empire. The still little-known literature of Muslim Albania withered in the late nineteenth century when the Albanians turned their backs on the Sublime Porte and strove to become an independent European nation. The solid beginnings of modern literature in the 1930s were weeded out ruthlessly by the Stalinist rulers who took power in 1944 and held on to it until 1990. Finally, the literature of Albanian socialist realism, which the Communist regime had created, became outdated, untenable, and unwanted the moment the dictatorship collapsed. Nonetheless, this tender plant has produced some stunning blossoms in that rocky and legendary soil, many of which merit the attention of the outside world.

For decades, and until quite recently, more poetry was printed and read in Albania and among the Albanians of the former Yugoslavia than all other literary genres combined. Is there a poet slumbering in every Albanian? Perhaps. Publishing statistics would certainly indicate a strong preference for verse over prose. In Tirana about 40 percent of literary publications in the 1990s were poetry, and in Prishtina at times up to 70 percent, something quite unimaginable in the rational West.

A nation of poets? When impoverished and ill-educated Albanian emigrants and refugees gather in Western Europe or in North America in their often dingy and always smoke-filled clubs, they most often congregate for a poetry reading. It is in poetry that the soul of the Albanian nation finds its expression. Albanian prose of high quality is admittedly a more recent phenomenon, and drama is still a much-neglected genre, but the Albanians have always spontaneously opened their hearts to lyrics.

This anthology is the first of its kind in English to present the full range of Albanian verse, from earliest times to the present day. The collection endeavors to be representative in that it showcases the works of the best-known and most-admired poets in the Albanian language. For the vibrantly prolific contemporary period, admittedly, it can provide no more than a sampling, yet it is to be hoped that this selection will suffice to reveal some of the preoccupations, concerns, and dreams of the writers of this fascinating part of southeastern Europe.

Robert Elsie

■ □ ■ □ ■

LIGHTNING FROM THE DEPTHS

■ □ ■ □ ■

ORAL EPIC POETRY

The Songs of the Frontier Warriors (*Këngë kreshnikësh*) are the best-known cycle of northern Albanian epic verse. Still sung by elderly men, while playing the one-stringed *lahuta*, these epic rhapsodies are the literary reflections of legends portraying and glorifying the heroic feats of warriors of the past. The main cycle, that of Mujo and Halili, preserves much of the flavor of other heroic cultures such as those mirrored in Homer's *Iliad* in Greek, *Beowulf* in English, *El Cid* in Spanish, the *Chanson de Roland* in French, the *Nibelungenlied* in German, and the Russian *byliny*. The leaders of this band of thirty *agas* (warriors) are Gjeto Basho Mujo and his brother Halili, who inhabit a frontier region between the Ottoman Empire and Austria-Hungary. The Albanian songs of Mujo and Halili parallel the Bosnian versions of the cycle sung in Serbo-Croatian, or more properly, Bosnian. This heroic and epic verse occurs in both oral literatures and cultures, since the singers in southern Bosnia, the Sandjak, and Montenegro at the time were largely bilingual, reciting alternatively in Bosnian and Albanian.

While the Bosnian Slav epic seems to have died out as a living tradition, the Albanian epic is still very much alive. Even as the twenty-first century marches on, one can still find a number of *lahutar*s in Kosova, in particular in the Rugova highlands west of Peja, and in northern Albania, and there are some rare souls in Montenegro who are able to sing and recite the heroic deeds of Mujo and Halili and their thirty *agas* as part of an unbroken oral tradition. One can safely assume that these elderly men constitute the very last traditional native singers of epic verse in Europe.

The Source of Mujo's Strength

Blessed we are, thanks to the Almighty!
For nothing we were until God did create us.
When Mujo was little, when he was a youngster,
His father dispatched him to work for a rich man.
The rich man did give him a job as a cowherd.

Day after day Mujo roamed the high pastures,
Day after day he would drink at the fountains,
Day after day in the shade took his leisure,
Not a trail or a pathway did he leave untrodden
To lead his herd onward to new mountain meadows.
But one night the cowherd lost sight of his cattle.
As he was unable to go home without them,
At the foot of a cliff he was forced to take refuge.
Here the young lad fell asleep for the nighttime.
Not far from the lad there were two cradles lying,
From both of the cradles emerged a faint whining.
Mujo approached to see what was inside them,
Mujo approached now to comfort the infants,
To comfort the infants by rocking their cradles
And lulling the little ones back into slumber.
Shining like lights stood before him two *zanas.*
"What are you doing?" they said, asking Mujo,
"Whatever compelled you to take this direction?"
Mujo then turned and to them gave his answer:
"I make my living up here as a cowherd,
Roaming for days on the high mountain pastures,
But this very day there occurred a misfortune,
My cattle have vanished and I cannot find them.
When darkness descended, I lay down to sleep here
But my eyes never closed because of the whining,
It was the whining I heard of two infants,
No peace of mind did their whimpering leave me,
Touched as I was, I got up to console them,
And giving them comfort, I got them to sleep.
But who are you beings in all of your splendor?"
"We are the *zanas,* Mujo, on our journey,
Giving to mankind our help and assistance.
And what favor do you ask of us, O Mujo,
For rocking our infants to sleep in their cradles?
Do you want strength, Mujo, to put up resistance?
Do you want might, Mujo, to fight in pitched battle?
Or do you, Mujo, desire goods and possessions?
Or do you want wisdom, to speak foreign tongues?

Tell us your wish and to you we will grant it."
Listen to how Mujo then turned and responded:
"The shepherds on many occasions have teased me,
For me they have only shown ire and derision,
Just give me strength so that I can outdo them."
The *zanas* took counsel at this and decided:
"Some milk from our breasts will we give unto Mujo."
And milk of their breasts they did give him to drink of,
Three drops were sufficient to nourish the young lad.
Such was the strength that the Lord did accord him
That he had the force to make lofty cliffs tremble.
"Take hold of that boulder," commanded the *zanas*,
A boulder that weighed more than one thousand *okas*.
Taking hold of the boulder of one thousand *okas*,
With his hands did he seize it and lift it a little,
Up to his ankles, no more could he raise it.
The *zanas* took counsel at this and decided:
"More of our milk we will offer to Mujo."
Mujo was given more milk and did drink it,
Again with his arms did he tackle the boulder,
And up to his knees this time managed to raise it,
And then to the ground for a rest let it plummet.
Heed now how nobly the *zanas* then offered:
"Let us again give our breasts unto Mujo."
Again from their breasts did they give milk to Mujo.
Such was the strength that the Lord did accord him
That the boulder once more with his arms he did grapple
And up to his waist did he manage to raise it.
The *zanas* were studying him and observing,
Again they took counsel at this and decided:
"Once more must we offer our breasts unto Mujo."
Mujo was offered their breasts and took milk there.
And such was the strength that the Lord gave him this time
That he seemed to acquire the strength of a *dragua*.
Mujo again with his arms seized the boulder,
And up to his shoulders did manage to raise it,
Holding suspended the one thousand *okas*.
And what did the *zanas* then say to each other?

"No more shall we give of our breasts unto Mujo.
For if we once more should provide them to Mujo
He'd likely take hold of the planet and squash it."
The *zanas* began to converse then with Mujo,
Speaking to him in their voices so gentle,
While over their heads shone the moon, which observed them,
And shadows were lengthening under the rock cliffs.
In cordial tones did the *zanas* address him,
Hear what the *zanas* did say unto Mujo:
"We wish you, O Mujo, to be our blood brother,
Speak up now, O Mujo, and give us your answer."
"Whenever I need you, O *zanas*, assist me!"
The Lord brought about the return of the daylight,
And Mujo awakened from out of his slumber,
And, finding his cattle, he drove the beasts homeward.
When Mujo got back to the Plain of Jutbina,
He noticed the shepherds had gathered together,
Preparing as always, as they were accustomed,
To make sport of Mujo by using their muscles.
Listen this time to how Mujo reacted.
Himself he began to make sport of the shepherds,
The mightiest one by the hand did he tackle
And into the air five good lengths did he hurl him.
None of them ventured to utter a protest,
For had he but touched them with his little finger,
They'd have been smashed to the ground and have perished.
Mujo abandoned the charge of his master
And, leaving his master, he turned and departed.
To his home he then traveled to visit his mother.
There, so they say, did Mujo start working,
There, so they say, did Mujo start fighting,
And from every battle that Mujo was part of,
He always emerged as a hero victorious.

Blessed we are, thanks to the Almighty!
For nothing we were until God did create us.
Daylight arrived and the sun began shining.
What was Gjeto Basho Mujo now doing?
Mujo had been to the Realm of the Christians
And there for himself a bride he'd selected,
It was the king's daughter whom Mujo had chosen.
When Mujo thereafter returned to Jutbina,
Three hundred wedding attendants he gathered,
With swords all glowing and with gilded garments,
With arrows and lances, in gold they were glinting,
Dapple-gray gleaming were all of their horses,
The attendants themselves were all youthful *agas*,
With one exception, the old man who led them,
Called by the name of Dizdar Osman Aga.
"Hear what I say now, O wedding attendants,"
Mujo arose and did speak to them, saying:
"When you get up to the high mountain pastures,
There you will find three broad shady meadows,
You must take care not to make merry on them,
You must take care not to strike up a carol,
You must take care not to lie down upon them,
For this is the home of the three fearsome *zanas*
Who surely have come to repose in the shade there,
To lie at their leisure amongst the cool breezes.
Well and alive they will let no one pass them!"
The light of the sun did come out the next morning,
The wedding attendants did saddle their stallions,
And getting up onto them, struck up a carol,
And they did make merry, while riding their horses,
There on their journey did sing and did revel,
Taking the road to the Realm of the Christians.
And when they got up to the high mountain pastures,
There they fell silent and held back their singing,
Gripped the reins firmly and guided their horses,
Nowhere did they stop but continued their journey,

None of them ventured to drink the springwater,
Nor did they rest in the shade of the meadows.
On to their host did they hasten their journey.
How warmly and heartily did the king greet them,
Food and drink did he bring forth so to feed them.
They struck up a carol and reveled 'til midnight.
When, once again, as the dawn came upon them,
They put on their boots and they put on their buckles,
The bride with them now, they set off on their journey,
Departing once more on the road to Jutbina.
Nowhere on their way did they silence their singing,
Nowhere on their way did they pause in their prancing,
Until they got up to the broad shady meadows,
There the old man to them spoke out, addressing:
"Hear what I say now, O wedding attendants.
For many a bride have I been an attendant,
And with all the brides have we always come hither
And taken our rest on these broad shady meadows,
The steeds every time we have put out to pasture,
And here in the shade have we struck up a carol,
And in these cool springs have we sought our refreshment,
Not once has a man of ours suffered misfortune!"
Then they all together dismounted their horses,
No longer sallying forth on their journey.
There did they stretch themselves out on the meadows,
There they made ready and struck up a carol,
There they began to make merry and revel,
There did they churn up and muddy the waters,
And all of their lances did launch at the targets.
Blessed we are, thanks to the Almighty!
While round about them the mountain peaks thundered,
The wind now did wail, through the beech trees it whistled,
And all of a sudden, in less than a second
Appeared there before them the three fearsome *zanas,*
Showing their teeth, they were snapping and snarling,
And out of their mouths there spewed fire and brimstone.
Then catching sight of the scene on the meadows,
At once did they turn to stone all of the revelers,

And all of their horses were turned into tree trunks,
All were transformed, just the bride was uninjured.
Grasping her arm did the *zanas* abduct her,
And seizing her, off to their cavern did steal her.
Nevermore was she able to sit or to rest there,
She cooked all their meals and fetched them their water.
Then of her plight heard Gjeto Basho Mujo,
Great was the fury that took hold of Mujo,
Onto the back of his courser jumped Mujo
And set off at once for the high mountain pastures.
When he arrived and was up on the meadows,
Thirty men frozen were what he discovered,
Turned there to stone were all thirty *agas*
And all of the steeds had been turned into tree trunks.
What pain and affliction now overcame Mujo!
Wasting no time, he then turned and departed,
Giving his courser no rest on the journey.
All by himself on the high mountain pastures,
Up at the springs did he search for the *zanas,*
Seeking and searching all over the meadows,
But nowhere was Mujo there able to find them.
Finally he looked in a forest of beech trees,
Where darkness holds sway and the light never enters,
Where no beam of sunlight is ever encountered,
There he discovered a fountain of water,
Sparkling and clear it was just like a teardrop,
Stopping there so he could find some refreshment,
Mujo jumped off of the back of his courser,
Casting his eyes at the grove all around him,
Nowhere was there a pathway to advance on,
Over the forest rose only the bare cliffs,
Below it were strewn naught but boulders and rubble,
So thick were the beech trees with all of their branches,
That no ray of sunlight had ever intruded.
Mujo then turned and did speak out, proclaiming:
"This surely must be the home of the *zanas.*"
Putting his steed in the grove out to pasture,
He sat himself down by the fountain and tarried,

Waiting to see when the *zanas* fetched water.
Later, when three days had passed and were over,
There journeyed a woman, a jug she did carry.
Mujo then pondered: Why, who is this woman,
And what is she doing in this lonely place here?
"Good day to you," did she then say to Mujo,
"Good day to you, too," did Mujo give answer.
   "What are you doing with the water?"
Inquired Mujo of the maiden.
"I don't know how to tell you, young man.
The wedding attendants came to fetch me,
And at a pleasant site we rested,
When there appeared three fearsome *zanas*.
For we'd been sitting at their tables,
Or from their sleep the *agas* woke them.
God knows what happened. I know only
The mountain peaks began to thunder,
The wind howled through the beechwood forest,
And three fearsome *zanas* stood before us.
'Neath shade they breathed upon the *agas*,
And made the horses into tree trunks,
Turned to stone were all the *agas*.
Seizing me, they took me with them
To make their meals and fetch their water!"
"To whom, O maiden, were you promised?
What's the name they use to call him?"
"I left my father, I left my mother,
I left my sisters, I left my brothers
To take as husband a great hero,
His name is Gjeto Basho Mujo!"
Straight-faced, Mujo then responded:
"If you saw him, would you know him?"
The maid replied again to Mujo:
"Wretched me, I would not know him,
For with my eyes I've never seen him,
From what I've heard, though, of the gossip,
You look like Gjeto Basho Mujo!"
How loudly Mujo burst out laughing:

"It's me, oh bride, who's here before you,
How easily you recognized me.
But, if you are a noble woman,
You'll listen now to what I tell you."
"By God, o'er sun and moon presiding,
I swear by the Lord of earth and heaven,
By him who brings us clouds and sunshine,
I will obey your words, O Mujo,
Though well I know they'd chop my head off!"
Mujo then began instructing:
"When you go back home this evening,
Approach, inquire of the *zanas:*
'By the meadows where you linger,
Where is it you get your power?'"
"Of their power will they tell me?"
Said the bride to Mujo, asking.
Mujo turned to her, responding:
"Do exactly as I've told you.
Behind the peaks the sun is setting,
The moon is shining through the beech trees,
In the moonlight will the *zanas*
Gather by the spring for dinner.
At the table they'll assemble,
But you must refrain from dinner.
The *zanas* will take pity on you.
Without you how could they eat dinner?
Use your wiles now and address them
And of their power they will tell you!
'By this meal,' you tell the *zanas,*
'By the peaks where you spend summer,
By the meadows where you linger,
By the fountains in your languor,
So much time I've spent now with you,
Won't you tell me of your power?'
If you survive, if they don't freeze you,
By your oaths, they're bound to answer.
You'll find me at the spring tomorrow."
The bride returned home through the forest,

Mujo left for the Green Valleys,
The maiden went back to the *zanas*,
"Where've you been so long?" they asked her.
"The waters at the spring were muddled,"
Murmured the maiden to the *zanas*.
They set the table, started eating,
The drinks were brought, they set to drinking.
She sliced them bread and brought them water,
But the bride refused to join them.
The little *zana* asked: "O sister,
Why are you not supping with us?
Are you ill and thus not hungry?"
"I shan't join you, little *zana*,
Nor will I share dinner with you
Unless you tell me of your power.
For an oath I now swear to you,
Though I'm a slave and you're the *zanas*,
And you can freeze me if you wish to:
By the peaks where you spend summer,
By the meadows where you linger,
By the fountains in your languor,
Tell me where you get your power."
Springing to their feet, the *zanas*
Pointed to the bride to freeze her.
Swiftly rose the little *zana*
And between them did she venture:
"May God damn you, O great *zana*,
Let us rather tell the maiden.
How could she do any damage?
Listen to me, human maiden,"
To the bride she turned, revealing:
"We rule over three wild he-goats,
On their heads are horns of ducats,
They inhabit the Green Valleys.
No one's ever caught the he-goats,
If they were to, would the power
We dispose of swiftly vanish!"
Down to dinner sat the maiden.

Sunlight did disperse the darkness,
The maiden set off for the fountain,
At the fountain she found Mujo.
Mujo gave a hearty chuckle:
"I see that you survived unfrozen."
"I survived, but all for nothing,
'Twas in vain you sent me to them,
From our dispute you've no profit,
They thus stated: 'We've three he-goats,
On their heads are horns of ducats,
They inhabit the Green Valleys,
No one's ever caught the he-goats.
If they were to, would the powers
We dispose of swiftly vanish!'"
Mujo turned to her, responding:
"You must go back to the *zanas*,
And pretend that nothing's happened.
Safe and sound will Mujo take you
Home with all the frozen *agas!*"
Up onto his steed he clambered,
Turning, set off for Jutbina,
Coming to Jutbina market,
He proclaimed to the *krahina:*
"All men here who count as hunters,
Take your hounds and get them ready,
Hasten to my house this evening,
Food and drink I'll furnish for you
And tomorrow we'll go hunting."
Three hundred hunters soon assembled,
With seven hundred hounds and further,
Three hundred hunting dogs were with them,
They all arrived at Mujo's doorway.
Mujo welcomed them and fed them.
When the light of dawn rejoined them,
Mujo turned to them, proclaiming:
"Listen to my words, O hunters,
We must take alive the he-goats.
There must be no mistake about it,

For if they're hunted down and slaughtered,
Will no one ever see Jutbina!"
With Mujo leading, they departed,
Journeyed up to the Green Valleys,
Round the valleys did they circle.
So Mujo was the first to enter
Three hundred hunting dogs were with him
As were the hounds, as were the hunters,
The other men arrayed in ambush.
Three full days and nights they hunted.
And when three days and nights were over,
The animals alive they'd captured.
Returning with them to Jutbina,
In a pen did Mujo keep them,
And he gave the hunters presents.
Thus vanished was the *zanas'* power,
They'd sought the goats but could not find them,
To the valleys they lamented,
To rocky cliffs loudly they cried out,
But nowhere could they hear their bleating.
Thereupon surmised a *zana:*
"Someone's robbed us of our he-goats!"
"Listen to me, mountain *zana,*"
Spoke the maid to the great *zana:*
"Mujo sends his greetings, saying:
'For the bride you've stolen from me,
For the wedding guests you've frozen,
Search no more for your wild he-goats,
Mujo's holding them as hostage!'"
When the *zanas* heard this message,
They departed for Jutbina,
Right to Mujo's door they journeyed.
"Have you taken our goats, Mujo?"
"I'm indeed the one who took them,
And in my pen have I confined them!"
The mountain *zana* now addressed him:
"We give up, Gjeto Basho Mujo,
Either in your home now slay us,

Or return to us the he-goats,
For we cannot live without them.
We'll unfreeze all the attendants,
We'll remit to you the horses,
Your bride we'll send to you by carriage."
Mujo cut them short, responding:
"The attendants that you mention
Do not really matter to me,
Nor do I long for the maiden,
In no time I'll find another,
But the goats I cannot give you
For such beasts I've never captured!"
At this they set about lamenting,
Gnashed their teeth and started weeping,
The very trees and rocks took pity.
But Mujo did remain undaunted.
To them turned the little *zana*
And with the hair upon her forehead
Wiped her tears and then touched Mujo.
A solemn oath she made him, swearing:
"Whenever you should go bride hunting,
Whenever you should fight a *baloz,*
When you set off with your fighters,
When you revel on our pastures,
When you wish to sing a song there,
When you shoot there at a target,
And use our springs for your refreshment,
Reposing in our shady meadows,
A solemn pledge do we now give you,
We'll say nothing to oppose you."
Such a promise melted Mujo.
Wasting no more time to ponder,
Mujo gave them formal answer:
"You are *zanas,* you'll be *zanas,*
Words are words and pledges, pledges.
I'll return you your wild he-goats.
Pluck them from the pen, Halili,"
Ordered Mujo of the youngster.

How the *zanas* changed expression
When they saw him free their he-goats!
In a twinkling they had vanished
Back up to the mountain pastures,
Finding there in the Green Valleys
All the petrified attendants,
And the horses turned to tree trunks.
Then they changed back the attendants,
Brought to life again the horses.
The maiden they put in a carriage,
And returned her to Jutbina.
When they reached the plain Jutbina,
All the maidens started singing,
The attendants started dancing,
All the mountain peaks resounded.
From cliff to cliff proclaimed the *zanas:*
"We are *zanas,* we'll be *zanas,*
Words are words and pledges, pledges,
We've brought back your bride and *agas.*"
From one cliff sang the great *zana,*
Little *zana* from another,
Hand in hand proclaimed the *zanas:*
"We are *zanas,* we'll be *zanas,*
Words are words and pledges, pledges,
A woman's a woman and a *zana's* a *zana,*
A *zana's* the sun and a woman's the moon.
Woe to the one who puts faith in a woman!"

Omer, Son of Mujo

It's you we worship, God Almighty!
The day had dawned, but little light shone,
The sun came up, no warmth provided,
Better had the light not come out,
Better had the sun not risen,
The two best *agas* were made prisoner,

Caught were Mujo and Halili,
At their fireplace they'd left no one,
Only Mujo's pregnant wife there,
God bestowed a son upon her,
And a fair name did they give him,
Called him Omer, son of Mujo.
When at the mere age of seven
Did he tower seven ells high,
On the scales weighed seventy *okas,*
And still the boy had not left home yet.
When he was seven, did his mother
Send him off to tend the goat kids,
That day he spent chasing a rabbit,
At night he hid it in the *kulla.*
Turning to his mother, he said:
"That gray goat kid, may God damn it,
Would not give me peace and quiet,
Come and light the pine torch, Mother,
For God has maybe slain the goat kid,
Let's check and see it in the cellar."
The mother went down to the goat kids
And there she saw a mountain rabbit.
The mother well knew what had happened,
Turning to the boy, she uttered:
"That, my son, is no gray goat kid,
That's a rabbit from the mountains!
But no matter, boy, I see that
It's your fate to be a hero!"
Omer one day told his mother:
"By the God who made me, Mother,
No father have I and no uncle?
Did you find me in the bushes?"
The mother swore to him, replying:
"You had a father and an uncle,
But perished both of them of smallpox,
They are buried in the garden."
The boy then swore to her, replying:
"Bring Halili's field glass, mother,

For I'll climb up to the tower,
And look out o'er field and meadow."
The mother brought Halili's field glass
And he climbed up to the tower,
Looked out to the distant hillocks,
Studied all the fields and meadows,
And gazed at the plains around him.
Turning to his mother, he said:
"By the God who made you, Mother,
What's that white thing on the meadows?
Could it be a snow-white landslide,
A ravine with rocks and gravel,
Or a flock of lambs with shepherds,
Or the *shkjas* with tent pavilions?"
The mother swore to him, replying:
"It's not the *shkjas* with tent pavilions,
It's the *agas* of Jutbina,
Daily there do they assemble."
Facing then his mother, he said:
"Bring Halili's garments, Mother,
Bring the saber for the war grounds,
Bring me also Mujo's courser,
For I'd like to meet the *agas*."
Hear his mother's words in answer:
"You are young, boy, and I'm frightened
That the *agas* will insult you,
Mujo'd often made them angry."
But Omer would just not listen.
She gave him armor, which he girded,
Snatched the saber for the war grounds,
Got the garments of Halili,
Perfectly the clothes did fit him.
Then she brought forth Mujo's courser,
When he tried to mount the courser,
He couldn't reach up to the crupper.
Then the steed he told in Turkish:
"A mighty courser they have called you,
Fall down on your knees before me

So that I can reach your crupper.
Down the road ride to Jutbina."
Like a storm the courser set off,
The *agas* of Jutbina heard it,
"What are all those peals of thunder?
Is a thunderstorm approaching?"
Then said Arnaut Osmani:
"It sounds like Mujo and Halili."
To his feet he rose to look out,
Saw but smoke and dust before him,
And in it Omer, son of Mujo.
Osmani glimpsed him with displeasure,
And turning to the *agas* swore out:
"It's the bastard son of Mujo,
Let none of us wish him welcome,
Let no one give word of greeting,
And no one put his horse to pasture."
When the lad got to the *agas,*
He with a *selam* did greet them,
But they gave no word of welcome,
No one offered that he sit down,
No one put his horse to pasture.
Only Zuku Bajraktari
Who was Mujo's true blood brother,
Gave the boy a word of greeting,
Had him sit among the others,
Put his fine horse out to pasture.
Omer then spoke to the meeting:
"Damn you," he addressed the *agas,*
"Why've you given me no greeting?
Nor a seat for me to sit on,
Nor put out my horse to pasture?
All of you well recognize me,
I'm son of Gjeto Basho Mujo,
Mujo's often made you angry,
But all the wars were won by Mujo,
Mujo's given you great honor,
Many of the *shkjas* he's slaughtered,

Protected you against great danger,
And not a bit of thanks you've shown him,
All you show him is your envy."
The *agas* murmured and took counsel,
Then they started their complaining:
"From the sea has come a *baloz*,
None of us will dare combat it,
Though it's claiming our possessions."
What said Omer, son of Mujo?
"Send a message to the *baloz*
To be early on the war grounds."
What did Osman Aga utter?
"If it's true you're really Omer,
Your father and uncle are in prison,
And from the prison you must free them
The king has held them seven years now,
Down in Kotor are they captive,
Their hair has grown long to the floorboards,
For seven years they've seen no sunlight,
For seven years no change of clothing,
For seven years no way of shaving."
At this, the boy could wait no longer,
He turned and jumped onto his courser,
And took the road that led him homeward.
Before the gateway of the *kulla*
He stopped and cried out to his mother:
"Stick your tit out of the window,
Because I need your breast, good mother!"
She stuck her tit out of the window,
With his left hand did he seize it,
With his right hand took his saber,
And swore by God unto his mother:
"Tell me where're my father and uncle,
Or I'll cut your tit to pieces."
The mother told her son in answer:
"The *agas* have been talking nonsense,
You're too young and they insult you.
You had a father and good uncle,

Both the king has taken prisoner,
Down in Kotor are they captive,
Their hair has grown long to the floorboards,
They're kept unwashed, no change of clothing,
I was too afraid to tell you,
For seven years I have not seen them."
What said Omer, son of Mujo?
"Bring Hungarian garments, Mother."
Hungarian garments did she bring him,
Sewed upon them Christian crosses.
Then he took his *sharki* with him,
Up he jumped onto his courser,
And he set off for the kingdom,
And the kingdom did he enter.
When he reached a village fountain,
He took his *sharki* and did play it,
Played with skill and sang out fairly.
Rusha, the king's daughter, heard him.
What did Omer now say to her?
"A cup of water, give me, Rusha,
From far and wide have I come traveling
In search of Father and my uncle."
The maiden swore to him, responding:
"To no one will I offer water,
Save to Omer, son of Mujo,
Seven years prior, God did make him,
Well the Seven Kingdoms know him."
The boy now, putting down his *sharki*,
Started asking Rusha questions,
Then did he reveal to Rusha:
"By the Lord on high who made me,
I am Omer, son of Mujo,
Here to free the two from prison,
Or I'll perish in the kingdom,
Tell me, maiden, how to do it!"
Rusha was in love with Omer
And proposed a plan to help him.
Of her plan did she tell Omer:

"Of twin sons the king is father,
They are fair lads who've no equals.
'Twould be easy to deceive them
And to bring them to the fountain,
Let them play here in the water.
If you from the king could catch them,
He'd free your father and your uncle."
Omer with this plan was happy,
From the king he seized the twin sons,
Took them with him on his courser.
With them traveled the king's daughter,
Singing as she journeyed with them,
The twins, however, traveled weeping.
With skill did Omer play his *sharki,*
Safe and sound they reached Jutbina,
All Jutbina feasted with them.
See what Omer then decided.
To the king he sent a warning:
"You who are king in your kingdom,
If you're missing any children,
Don't waste time to try and find them,
For they're held in Omer's prison.
Free my father and my uncle
Or I'll tear your twins to pieces."
The king then saw he was in trouble,
Forthwith to his feet he sprang up,
And to the prison door he hastened:
"Come out, Mujo, may God damn you,
For my twins your son has captured,
They lie day and night in prison,
He says he might chop their heads off."
"By the God who did create me,
I will only leave this prison
When I'm kempt and when I'm shaven."
Swiftly were the barbers summoned
And just as swiftly did they shave him.
"Come out, Mujo, may God damn you."
"By the God who did create me,

I will only leave this prison
When I get well-folded fabrics,
And three donkeys with gold laden."
Swiftly did the king give orders,
On two mares he piled red fabrics,
On three donkeys loaded money,
Burdened were they full of gold coins.
"Come out, Mujo," did he holler,
"Alive I'll not come out," said Mujo,
"Unless you give my son your Rusha,
And me a tray of golden ducats!"
What was it the king responded?
"You both today will be my in-laws,
The boy shall take as bride my Rusha!"
Then the heroes left their prison,
And departed for Jutbina.
When they finally reached their *kulla*,
Hear what Mujo told Halili:
"When I go into the *kulla*
Will I seize the twins to slay them,
For today I'll meet my Omer.
Should the lad be my son really,
He'll not let me slay the twin boys."
With one hand he seized the twin sons,
With the other seized his saber,
When he was about to slay them,
His son jumped to his feet, protesting,
Arming himself for a battle,
That his guests should not be slaughtered.
The two men set upon each other,
But in harmony they parted,
Throwing arms around each other,
"Hail, my boy, that I now see you,
And you really are my true son."
To the king they sent the twin boys,
And then held a celebration
That they'd lived to be united.

Gjergj Elez Alia

Gjergj Elez Alia, the greatest of heroes,
For nine years now on his bed has he languished,
Night and day one sister stays at his bedside,
Cleansing his wounds for nine years with springwater,
Cleansing his wounds all the time with her teardrops,
And wiping the blood with the locks of her long hair,
She bound his wounds in the shawl of their mother,
Their father's old garments protected his body,
Down at the foot of the bed hung his weapons.
Each night when tucked into his bed by his sister,
He weaned his thoughts off of his body's discomfort,
But writhed with the pain he had caused to his sister.
Rumor was spreading and it became known that
A swarthy *baloz* had emerged from the ocean.
The monster was evil and bent on destruction,
From all of the regions he claimed heavy tribute:
"Each household shall give me a whole roast of mutton,
Each household shall render to me a fine maiden,
Day after day a *kreshnik* must be slaughtered,
And week after week must be ravaged a region."
Soon it was Gjergj who received the injunction,
The cheeks of her brother were covered in teardrops,
How could he cede to the *baloz* his honor?
Now did the sister start keening and wailing,
With tears in her eyes, then to Gjergj she lamented:
"Death has forgotten to take us, dear brother,
With mother and father lying far 'neath a linden,
And you for nine years have been chained to your bedstead.
Your sister, must she to the *baloz* be ceded?
Why doesn't the *kulla* collapse and destroy us,
Why doesn't our tower turn into a tombstone,
Protecting and keeping your honor untarnished?"
Gjergj was heartbroken at hearing her grieving,
And opened his eyes, contemplating his sister.
The cheeks of the hero were streaming with teardrops,
And speaking out now, did he rage at the *kulla:*

"O fortress of mine, may you blacken, grow dismal,
And may you be rotten from top down to bottom,
May you for tenants have serpents and vipers.
How have you let the floors dampen with raindrops?"
"No, my dear brother," responded the sister,
"You don't understand, the fever's confused you,
It hasn't been raining at all, my dear brother,
It's simply the tears of your sister you're seeing!"
Gjergj took the hand of his sister and squeezed it,
Stroking her arm with his firm solid fingers,
He looked at his sister, her eyes full of sorrow,
With words clear and lucid did he now address her:
    "My good sister, why the weeping?
Why do you tear my heart asunder?
For nine full years now have I quivered
Like the beech trees in the sunlight,
No respite have I been given,
But tell me, has your brother ever
Of clothes, food, water e'er deprived you?
Has your brother ever cursed you,
Or let his anger out upon you
That you'd rather leave and marry?"
How well answered now the sister,
While his hand was on her forehead:
    "Why do you speak so, my burgeoning beech tree?
Perchance has the fever got hold of your senses?
I'd rather be buried alive than be married,
You've never deprived me of food or of water,
And never begrudged me fine garments and footwear,
And never more harshly than now have you spoken,
Other than you I've no father or mother,
I beg you, my brother, do not be offended
By all of the worries I'm to you confessing.
Nine springtimes have passed and your body remains here,
You've never got up and gone out of the doorway.
And not a complaint have you heard from your sister,
But should I thus give myself now to the *baloz*?"
The hero then rose to his feet and gave orders:

"Go and fetch my warhorse, woman,
And make your way straight to the city,
Find the farrier, my blood brother,
Tell him Gjergj does send him greetings,
Let him ready brassy horseshoes,
And with nails of steel do fit them,
For the *baloz* shall I challenge!
And should the farrier not be willing,
Take it to my friend, the blacksmith."
The maid then set out for the city,
To find the farrier, his blood brother:
"Success and greetings to you, brother!"
"And to you greetings, distant sister!"
"To you does Gjergj convey his greetings,
And begs you fit and shoe the courser,
Do make ready brassy horseshoes,
And with nails of steel do fit them,
For the *baloz* he will challenge."
Slyly spoke the farrier brother:
"If you give me, maid, your favors,
I'll ensure your brother's triumph
And wings to fly I'll give his courser!"
Oh, what fury seized the maiden:
"How dare you, man, may your tongue wither,
I thought I'd come to our blood brother,
The steed's not been here for nine years now,
And you behave like some lewd gypsy,
For I'm devoted to my parents
Who are rotting in the graveyard,
And to poor Gjergj, gravely weakened!"
To the blacksmith rode the sister:
"To you does Gjergj convey his greetings,
It's his turn now to do battle,
As best you can, please shoe the courser,
Do make ready brassy horseshoes,
And with nails of steel do fit them,
For the sea *baloz* he'll challenge."
As if 'twere his, he shod the courser.

Returning home, the maiden found Gjergj
Waiting, shaded by a linden.
What of the hero, Gjergj Alia?
He'd sent his greetings to the *baloz,*
To meet him early at the war grounds.
"I've no maiden for you, *baloz,*
My sheep have not been fattened for you,
I've but one sister, not to give you,
Who else would bind my injured body?"
When the dawn first lit the mountains,
To the war grounds came the heroes,
And began exchanging insults:
"From the grave, Gjergj, have you risen?
Why've you called me to the war grounds?"
Wisely did the hero answer:
   "I well understand, haughty words have you spoken.
Nine years have gone by that I've been on death's doorstep,
But you have revived me now with your arrival.
You demanded my sister before doing battle,
You wanted my sheep without asking the shepherd,
Now I have come to the war grounds to teach you
An ancient tradition we've from our forefathers,
Without rendering arms there is nothing we'll give you,
Never to you will I render my sister,
Without doing battle before on the war grounds,
Your day has come, *baloz,* so make yourself ready."
Thus spoke his challenge Gjergj Elez Alia,
They spurred on their steeds and they rushed into battle,
The *baloz* stormed forth and attacked with his cudgel,
Down to its knees tumbled Gjergj's swift courser,
And over their heads did the cudgel spin past them,
Twenty-four yards flying into the valley,
Twenty-four yards in the air rose the dust cloud,
Now it was his turn for Gjergj to do battle.
Skillfully pivoting, he hurled his cudgel,
Through the air did it hurtle and struck down the *baloz.*
The *baloz* collapsed and the earth gave a shudder.
In barely a moment did Gjergj draw his saber,

And heaving it, severed the head from the body,
The torso he dragged by the feet then behind him
And hurtled it into a lake from his courser,
The river flowed black with the blood of the monster,
And for three whole years it infested the region.
The victor then turned and went back to his *kulla,*
And there he assembled all of his companions.
"Take counsel, companions, in what I now tell you,
To you do I offer my tower and fortress,
To you I bequeath and bestow all my money,
All my belongings and all of my cattle,
And assign you the sister of Gjergj Elez Alia."
The hero then turned and in one final effort
Threw his arms round the neck of his unlucky sister,
At that very moment the two hearts ceased beating,
Dead to the ground fell both brother and sister,
No better spirits have ever been rendered.
His friends began mourning in great lamentation,
And for the two siblings a wide grave dug open,
For brother and sister, their arms round each other,
And over the grave did they make a fair tombstone,
That brother and sister would not be forgotten,
And there, at the headstone they planted a linden,
A place of repose for the birds in the summer.
And when in the spring the hills broke into blossom,
A cuckoo flew by and reposed on the gravestone
And found that the twigs of the linden had withered.
Then it took flight to the tenantless tower,
And found that the rooftop had fallen to ruins.
Winging, it landed on one of the windows,
And called from its perch to a wanderer passing,
"O wanderer passing by into the mountains,
Should you be singing, please cease for a moment,
Should you be crying, then mourn and lament here,
For I have searched o'er the high mountain pastures,
For I have flown o'er the low winter meadows,
For I have wandered from house to house weeping,
I nowhere could find him, Gjergj Elez Alia!"

■ □ ■ □ ■

EARLY ALBANIAN VERSE

PJETËR BUDI
1566–1622

Pjetër Budi, known in Italian as Pietro Budi, was born in the village of Gur i Bardhë in the Mat region of the north-central Albanian mountains. At the age of twenty-one he was ordained as a Catholic priest and sent immediately to Macedonia and Kosova, then part of the ecclesiastical province of Serbia under the jurisdiction of the archbishop of Antivari (Bar), where he served in various parishes for an initial twelve years. In 1610 he is referred to as "chaplain of Christianity in Skopje" and in 1617 as "chaplain of Prokuplje." In 1616, Budi traveled to Rome, where he resided until 1618 to oversee the publication of the four religious prose works in Albanian for which he is remembered. In 1621, he was made bishop of Sapa and Sarda (Episcopus Sapatensis et Sardensis), that is, of the Zadrima region, and he returned to Albania the following year. In December 1622 he drowned while crossing the Drin River.

Budi seems to be the first writer from Albania to have devoted himself seriously to poetry and is author of the earliest-known verse in the Gheg dialect. His works include some 3,300 lines of religious verse, almost all in quatrain form with an alternate rhyme. Though Budi's verse is not without style, its content, being imitations of Italian and Latin moralist verse of the period, is not particularly original. He prefers biblical themes, eulogies, and universal motifs such as the inevitability of death. What is attractive in Budi's verse is the authenticity of feeling and genuine human concern for the sufferings of a misguided world.

O Hapless, Luckless Man

"Here I wish to say a few words on the subject of Death, vanity, and the ingratitude of man."

O hapless, luckless man,
Forever lost in evil,
Giv'n over to conceit, and
Dazed, in sin enveloped.

Be you young or be you old,
Be you lord or be you servant,
Why can't you see and fathom
The mire that you are made of?

You're black soil and you're mud,
And not of gold a-sparkling,
You're not sprung from the angels,
Nor carved of cherished jewels.

Whence does your strength derive
In vanity to revel,
The good Lord, to oppose him
In all his glorious splendor?

Your own renown alone
You beheld and acknowledged,
When born into this world,
Forsaken by your mother.

With you appeared no wealth,
No riches, lavish treasures,
No wisdom, knavish cunning,
No values, precious gemstones.

With you appeared no greatness,
You had no gift for speaking,
No courage and no virtue,
And nothing to assist you.

With you appeared no bearing,
No swift and handsome horses,
No bloodline and no family,
No good you've brought or evil.

For you were birthed defiled,
Forsaken by your mother,
And in a venomed clamor
You cried out in your longing.

For this was all you knew,
You had naught to assist you.
You had no gift for speaking,
All filthy and all sullied.

All you could do was wail,
And in a venomed clamor
You offered nothing more
Than futile lamentation.

You came into this world
To suffer but affliction,
Your tears flowed, arrows pierced you,
With hostile men encircled.

You're full of wrath, and bitter,
Exposed and sore neglected,
The life that you are leading
Is but that of a prisoner.

The Deed of Cain

Vile hound, what have you done
By that bloody deed committing?
May the earth, when it espies you,
Hide in darkness and in mourning.

May all your efforts fail,
May your wishes be frustrated,
May seed on your fields wither
And no fruit grow ripe to harvest.

When first your mouth you opened,
Your brother's blood imbibing,
With your own hands you slew him,
And the crime did heaven witness!

The skies were torn asunder,
And through the void you wandered,
Both day and night a-weeping,
And death your eyes envisioned.

Ceaseless, searching ever
Like a wild beast in the wasteland,
Dazed do you now wander,
Mad dog upon this planet.

LEKË MATRËNGA
1567–1619

Lekë Matrënga, known in Italian as Luca Matranga, was an Ortho-
dox cleric of the Italo-Albanian community of Sicily. He was also
the author of the second major work of early Albanian literature,
Christian Doctrine (*Embsuame e chraesterae* [Rome, 1592]), which is a
twenty-eight-page catechism translated from the Latin. Matrënga's
work contains an introduction in Italian—the catechism itself—
religious instruction on church doctrines in the form of questions
and answers, and an eight-line poem, which constitutes the earliest
specimen of written verse in Albanian.

Spiritual Song

I call you all who wish indulgence,
All good Christians, men and women,
Go to mass, the Lord commands it,
For no man is sinless 'mongst us;
Blithe is he who ponders God
And remembers he is mortal,
Christ will welcome him to heaven
With his children and his brethren.

PJETËR BOGDANI
ca. 1630–1689

Pjetër Bogdani, known in Italian as Pietro Bogdano, is the most
original writer of early literature in Albania. He is the author of the
Band of the Prophets (*Cuneus prophetarum* [1685]), the first prose work
of substance written originally in Albanian. Born in Gur i Hasit,
near Prizren, about 1630, Bogdani was educated in the traditions of
the Catholic Church, to which he devoted all his energy. From 1654
to 1656, he studied at the College of the Propaganda Fide in Rome,
where he graduated as a doctor of philosophy and theology. In 1656,
he was named bishop of Shkodra, a post he held for twenty-one
years, and was also appointed administrator of the archdiocese of
Antivari (Bar), a position he occupied until 1671. In 1677, he suc-
ceeded his uncle as archbishop of Skopje and administrator of the
Kingdom of Serbia.

The *Band of the Prophets* is considered to be the masterpiece of
early Albanian literature and is the first work in Albanian of full ar-
tistic and literary quality. In his work we encounter for the first time
what may be considered an Albanian literary language. As such, he
may justly bear the title of father of Albanian prose. His religious
poetry is, nonetheless, not devoid of interest. The corpus of his verse
is the *Songs of the Ten Sibyls* (the Cumaean, Libyan, Delphic, Per-
sian, Erythraean, Samian, Cumanian, Hellespontic, Phrygian, and

Tiburtine); these poems are imbued with the baroque penchant for
religious themes and biblical allusions.

The Cumaean Sibyl

Peace and abundant fruit will there be from heaven
For six years before his birth and, thereafter,
For another six will it know no end on earth.
O wonder! For the wolf, the sheep, and the lamb will dine
Together; the Son of Man and the dragon will live
Side by side without fear, without tears, or cries, or lamentation;
The lynx will spare the goats and kids,
For our Lord will guard and raise them in peace.

The Libyan Sibyl

He arrives as a man among mortal men,
To save the world with his own death
And passing by, to heal wounds with no balm,
To give sight to eyes, hearing to ears,
Proper movement to lame legs, without payment, without gold,
Expelling idols and the reign of death among us;
An only son, loved by his Mother,
Returned from the grave, safe and sound,
Clothed by the sun and shod by the moon,
A crown of stars circling his head.
The Maiden Mary, fairer than a *zana,*
Will receive her tender lad Jesus in her arms
To the envy of the Jews and the pagans
Who, plotting in council together,
Set forth to expel the lad Jesus,
Giving him no respite nor earthly place.

The Delphic Sibyl

I weep, wretched me, a loud lament
For Christ lying on the ground, drubbed and badly disfigured,
Given lashes, beatings, poison, and vinegar,
His body wound-battered and besmirched,
Israel on earth left no iniquity undone.
With a spear still piercing his head,
They laid him lifeless in the lap of his mother,
Rending her heart to pieces.

The Persian Sibyl

A voice from the mountains cries out in the wilderness
To carry the Gospel, to pave for the world the path
Of righteousness, to preach forgiveness of sins,
And baptism. In this life it will bring salvation
To those who renounce lies and deception.
They will find their place in paradise, if they so wish,
By crushing the head of that inner beast,
By doing good deeds and by going often to church.

The Erythraean Sibyl

Thus sings and writes the Ionian Sibyl:
The blazing wind from the heavens burns trees and stones,
Spreading throughout the world,
Instead of water, the springs well with blood,
So arid is it that even the seas dry up
As the world is consumed like a torch,
Emerging from the clouds, Christ on high
Descends irately to expel evildoers below,

PJETËR BOGDANI

Many wretches there suffer badly,
Seared to ashes their souls, flesh, and bones,
They and their cohorts pay the price for having done evil,
Sulfur, tar, and lead all combined,
Snow and ice are laid in their beds,
And never are they allowed to leave,
Forever and ever, inconsolable pain,
Forgotten by our Lord and the saints,
Damned be their idols, Muhammad, prophet of Allah,
Calvin, and Luther who deceived them,
May they be consigned to serpents and toads,
May the she-wolf consume for her meal the hearts
Of those who have trifled with hell,
Who have eaten meat on a Friday, day of fasting,
And you who unthinkingly have abandoned the faith,
Gullible, you have fallen for lies,
Pay attention to where you may be heading,
Yes, repent in this life,
Confessing your vain undertakings,
O Man, what you have accomplished are but arrows,
Illusion, jealousy, and envy. Weep for yourself.

The Samian Sibyl

O Zion, loftier than Pashtrik, mountain of Prizren,
We worship you, for from you will emerge the law.
When gentle Christ gave sweet pleasure to the apostles
With beloved communion and holy sermons,
And the Maiden, sent to you from on high,
Gave birth to the Son of Man, who taught us,
Then the Jews, who took your Godhead, meant for them,
Planted on his head a crown of thorns.

The Cumanian Sibyl

As Isaiah says, before the stem opens,
The infant flower shall come forth out of the root of Jesse,
Like a white lily in the springtime,
Or as a hyacinth in April sprouts from the earth,
God himself promised this to us many times,
The ancient synagogue will free itself of the knot,
Assuming a pure name fashioned of words.
Thus sings and speaks our Sibyl in verse.

The Hellespontic Sibyl

The Father gives birth to the Son in his own image,
The two, with the beloved Holy Ghost, breathe
Upon the world for its salvation, which conveys grace.
Whosoever wishes to see heaven, may he thus worship the Divine
And be freed of all his sins.
In his heart and on his brow may he honor the Cross
Upon which the second figure of the Trinity
Was nailed, overwhelmed by this life.

The Phrygian Sibyl

When blessed Christ perished, covered with wounds,
Stones and trees fractured, and the temple's canopy split in two,
Darkness shrouded the earth for three days,
The sun and the moon were both bathed in blood,
The heart of the world groaned in sorrow.
Many souls veiled themselves in flesh, and then,
After three days, they rose to heaven with Christ,
If any have done evil, then later they will suffer.

PJETËR BOGDANI

The Tiburtine Sibyl

After burying the Old Testament itself,
And leaving death and slavery behind him,
Like a lofty eagle, Christ crossed over to heaven.
Written in his own blood for you, O Man,
He illuminated paradise, and comforted all souls,
Promising to return later,
With all the saints, swathed in light,
To judge in righteousness good and evil.

■ □ ■ □ ■

POETRY IN THE MUSLIM TRADITION

NEZIM FRAKULLA

ca. 1680–1760

Nezim Frakulla, alternatively known as Nezim Berati or Ibrahim Nezimi, was the first major poet among the Bejtexhinj, popular poets in the Muslim tradition who wrote in Albanian but used Arabic script. He was born in the village of Frakull, near Fier, and lived a good deal of his life in Berat, a flourishing center of Muslim culture at the time. Frakulla studied in Istanbul, where he wrote his first poetry in Turkish, Persian, and perhaps Arabic, including two divans. About 1731, he returned to Berat, where he is known to have been involved in literary rivalry with other poets of the period, notably Mulla Ali, mufti of Berat. Between 1731 and 1735 he composed a divan and various other poetry in Albanian, including an Albanian-Turkish dictionary in verse form. Although we do not possess the whole of the original divan, we do have copies of about 110 poems from it. Some of his verse was put to music and survived the centuries orally, and the authorship is uncertain for a few of the poems ascribed to him. Frakulla asserts that he was the first person to compose a divan in Albanian.

Frakulla's divan includes verse ranging from panegyrics on local pashas and military campaigns to odes on friends and patrons, poems on separation from and longing for his friends and (male) lovers, descriptions of nature in the springtime, religious verse, and, in particular, love lyrics. The imagery of the latter ghazal, some of which are devoted to his nephew, is that of Arabic, Persian, and Turkish poetry, with many of the classical themes, metaphors, and allusions: love as an illness causing the poet to waste away, the cruel lover whose glance could inflict mortal wounds, or the cupbearer whose beauty could reduce his master to submission.

I'm Your Slave, You Are My Love

I'm your slave, you are my love,
I turn to you, my beloved,
Save me now or let me perish,

Take and choose the best solution,
I lament and am in torment,
Heavy on me lies this planet,
I to perish would prefer
And save myself from love's affliction.
Yet in spite of all our anguish,
Will our lovers not address us,
We are slaves in desolation,
Let them fetch us and dispatch us.

Oh, Your Gaze, That Slicing Saber

Oh, your gaze, that slicing saber,
And your eyes, those of a hero,
This, my life's become a prison,
. . . .

Your two locks are like two dragons,
All the others cower, fear you,
Like the autumn leaves they quiver,
Cringe before you, dauntless hero.

Meeting you made life eternal,
Separation's got me jealous,
Night and day I seek salvation,
Begging one more time to see you.

In your harshness I take pleasure,
In your glance, I find salvation,
Yearning for you is my illness,
None else on earth do I long for.

O my love, Nezim's religion,
Perfect beauty, Nezim's logic,
You are Nezim's balm and healing,
Life without you is but heartache.

Friends of Mine, They Are Fine Fellows

Friends of mine, they are fine fellows,
Good men who keep their word and promise,
When they saw that I was jailed
Each strove to come there and replace me.

A true friend in this world is one
Who gives you love and will support you,
When he sees you locked in prison
He will share the heavy burden.

A friend is one I know on earth
Who when he sees that you're in trouble,
If he cannot save you from it,
He will drown, too, in the ocean.

Not like this are other fellows,
Who your stewed prunes seize and gobble,
Turn, Nezim, now, look away
And do not long for their affection.

God in heaven, God of mercy!
Better there's no interjection,
Tribulation in this world will
Rob you of your peace and quiet.

Let me be as fate will have it,
I'll not groan in lamentation,
My one hope on earth is that I'll
Not on others be dependent.

NEZIM FRAKULLA

Nezim Has Made It Merry

Who bade the divan speak Albanian?
Nezim has made it known.
Who bade clarity speak in Albanian?
Nezim has made it human.

This language was in ruins,
Veiled in grief and shame.
Full well this book now proves it,
Nezim has made it merry.

A man upon this planet
Will never love possess
If he does not perceive this,
Nezim has made it marvel.

For a man in tears and anguish
From the pain of love, O friend,
By God now, with this verse
Nezim has made it sultan.

The grace of God is present
In the ecstasy of beauty,
And the troubling task of love songs,
Nezim has made it easy.

But do not say, companion,
That the lover speaks this tongue,
Look, the pathway once untrodden,
Nezim has made it open.

If a man is wise and cultured,
And takes and reads my poem,
This divan of pearls and jewels,
Nezim's made it his friend.

In the Dust Left by Your Footsteps

Listen to me, my beloved,
No peace do I find without you,
Life with you is like a rosebud,
When you're absent, life is sinful.

Thus it is and thus will e'er be,
No joy knows my heart without you,
And my body, may it wither
In the dust left by your footsteps.

You're my soul and you're my spirit,
I am but a wretched body,
You're my remedy and vigor,
I've lost pride and reputation.

I'm so in love, you hold my heart,
I'm nightingale, you're bow'r of roses,
You are spring, I'm flower garden,
You're the perfume I respire.

You are Leila, I am Mexhnun,
You're the doctor, I'm the patient,
I am gold, and you're alchemy,
I'm confusion, you are order.

I am Ferhad, you are Shirin,
You're a falcon, I'm a rock dove,
I am Muslim, you are Islam,
I'm the faithful, you are imam.

You're my king, and I'm the beggar,
You're my moon, and I am nighttime,
You're the dawn, and I await you,
You're the twilight, I am evening . . .

NEZIM FRAKULLA

I'm your slave and you're the master,
You're the guardsman, I'm your saber,
I'm the ball, and you're the striker,
I'm the bird whose heart you've captured . . .

Of my life you are the river,
On this planet I am Hizir,
You're fulfillment of my longing,
I'm the slave who begs for mercy . . .

You're my whim and my desire,
You're my mystery and secret,
I am Hafiz of Shiraz, and
I'm the Sa'adi of our lifetime.

You're the treasure of compassion,
I am both Said and Shevket,
You're the rainfall of my mercy,
I'm a shell of nacre shining.

Some Young Fellows Have Now Turned Up

Some young fellows have now turned up,
Shouting: "Why don't we be poets?"
Weep ye trees and weep ye boulders!
For the gems that they are penning.

True verse is God's inspiration,
It's no clotted cream for swilling,
Worry not, scent of the lily,
For by force is naught accomplished.

Pay attention, listen to me,
Let me tell you, if you're clever,
That these flowers are not easy,
They're not flags out in the pastures.

You can't understand a writer,
You don't know what he is saying,
Yet you sit there, trying to tell me
What it's like to be a poet.

God! their verse, where has it come from?
I must say, it is quite silly,
O Nezim, praise be upon you
For the jeweled words you've spoken.

We Have Set Off into Exile

We have set off into exile,
May the Lord on us have mercy,
And protect us on our journey,
Farewell to Berat of roses!

Istanbul, accept our greetings,
Can you find a space here for us?
Just enough and not too little,
For myself and these fine fellows.

Of our old friends we've one favor,
That they on our souls take pity,
Now and then they say a prayer,
May it be a blessing to them.

Friends of old, do not forget us,
For we're off to foreign countries,
Send salute and greetings to us
Every three, four months, we beg you.

May your wishes be accomplished
By the Lord in his compassion,
And, Nezim, O wretched fellow,
May He also hear you praying.

NEZIM FRAKULLA

I've one favor now to ask you,
Hail for me those fields and mountains,
To them convey my best wishes,
Greetings from me in my sorrow.

Tell them that Nezim is weeping,
With an open heart he begs you,
Set aside a venue for him,
Or he'll languish in perdition.

MUÇI ZADE
ca. 1724

Muçi Zade is the author of the earliest-known Albanian poem writ-
ten in Arabic script and in the Muslim tradition. The work is taken
from a manuscript discovered in Korça and is dated 1724. In this oc-
tosyllabic poem, with an *aaab* rhyme scheme in the Albanian origi-
nal, the author laments not having any coffee with which to break
his fast at sunset in the holy month of Ramadan. Nothing else is
known of the elderly Muçi Zade.

Lord, Don't Leave Me Without Coffee

By the wonders of the prophets,
By the saints that we acknowledge,
Let me break no fast a-thirsting,
Lord, don't leave me without coffee.

By the honor of Fatima,
And Meyreme, don't reject me
With a plate of salty yogurt,
Lord, don't leave me without coffee. . . .

Lord, don't let me break my fast with
Naught to eat but syrup, honey,
O God, you are my salvation,
Lord, don't leave me without coffee.

In the holy month we're marking,
Please forgive our sins, we're old folk,
By the angels up in heaven,
Lord, don't leave me without coffee.

By the one whose name means mercy,
By Muhammad, fame be to him,
Don't desert me with hulled barley,
Lord, don't leave me without coffee.

To the Lord prays Muçi Zade,
For he wallows in much woe with
Neither rice nor tapioca,
Lord, don't leave me without coffee!

HASAN ZYKO KAMBERI
d. early nineteenth century

Hasan Zyko Kamberi was born in the second half of the eighteenth
century in Starja, a southern Albanian village near Kolonja at the
foot of Mount Grammos. Of his life we know only that he took part
in the Turkish-Austrian Battle of Smederevo, on the Danube east
of Belgrade, in 1789 (AH 1203) in an army under the command of
Ali Pasha Tepelena (1741–1822). He died a dervish, no doubt of the
Bektashi sect, in his native village at the beginning of the nineteenth
century. His tomb, in Starja, was turned into a shrine known locally
as the turbeh of Baba Hasani.

Kamberi is one of the most commanding representatives of the
Muslim tradition in Albanian literature, though his main work, a
two-hundred-page *mexhmua* (verse collection), has disappeared. Of

the works we do possess are a short *mevlud*, a religious poem on the birth of the prophet Muhammad, about ten *ilâhî* (religious hymns), and over fifty secular poems. Kamberi's secular verse covers a wide range of themes. The most famous of his poems is "Money," a caustic condemnation of feudal corruption and at the same time perhaps the best piece of satirical verse in pre-twentieth-century Albanian literature.

Money

The sultan who rules the world,
The founder of the mint,
The place where silver's coined,
He knows what money's worth.

The vizier, who's his aide,
Who acts as if he's just,
He lets no gossip spread,
He knows what money's worth.

Sheyhulislami issues fatwas,
He knows what's canon law,
Yet a bribe he'll not refuse,
He knows what money's worth.

The mufti and the teacher,
Both scholars and imams,
Are in the devil's pact,
They know what money's worth.

The judge, too, in his courtroom,
Reclining on his rug,
The dervish in his tekke,
They know what money's worth.

The pashas and the beys
And all the milling crowds
For riches lose their heads,
They know what money's worth.

Show money to a judge,
He'll interpret laws anew,
For a cent he'd sell his father,
He knows what money's worth.

For money they'll get drunk
And put the world to shame,
E'en the farmer sowing beans,
He knows what money's worth.

There is no creature living
Exempt from this desire,
All guildsmen and all merchants,
They know what money's worth.

The infant in his cradle,
His hand out, crying "Gimme!"
Will cram cash in his pocket,
He knows what money's worth.

The jackdaw perched in silence,
Throw a penny on the ground,
'twill seize it, take it nestward,
It knows what money's worth.

Money in this world
Will consume both young and old,
In hellfire it will burn them,
They know what money's worth. . . .

HASAN ZYKO KAMBERI

Trahaná

All comrades, men and women,
Good people on this planet,
Praise and glory to him
Who invented *trahaná*.

What a blessing to the famished,
Mixing milk with flour and yogurt.
Praise and glory to him
Who invented *trahaná*.

He was, 'tis true, a wise man,
Was indeed no infant spirit,
Praise and glory to him
Who invented *trahaná*.

For eight months it is eaten,
Keeps alive the poorest people,
Praise and glory to him
Who invented *trahaná*.

In the morning when they waken,
Young and old for it do clamor,
Praise and glory to him
Who invented *trahaná*.

All the serfs and wretched bondsmen,
With their herds toiling and farming,
Praise and glory to him
Who invented *trahaná*.

In the huts where it is lacking,
Do the children mewl, O mercy,
Praise and glory to him
Who invented *trahaná*.

No other food can match it,
Like wine it soothes the stomach,
Praise and glory to him
Who invented *trahaná*.

With milk is it enfolded
And with butter pan-browned, scalded,
Praise and glory to him
Who invented *trahaná*.

Into your bowl you put it
And with bread, black pepper, taste it,
Praise and glory to him
Who invented *trahaná*.

Trahaná is an honor
And a treat when boiled and steamy,
Praise and glory to him
Who invented *trahaná*.

HASAN ZYKO KAMBERI

■ □ ■ □ ■

ITALO-ALBANIAN VERSE

NICOLA CHETTA
1742–1803

Italo-Albanian writer and poet Nicola Chetta (Nikollë Keta) was born in Contessa Entellina (Kundisa), the oldest Albanian settlement in Sicily, founded between 1450 and 1467. He was educated at the Greek seminary in Palermo, becoming, in 1777, its rector. As a poet, he wrote both religious and secular verse in Albanian and Greek, and he has the honor of having composed the first Albanian sonnet.

Of Honorable Lineage

Of honorable lineage in Contessa was born
Nic Chetta, a scion of the Albanian soil.
He went to Palermo, to the Albanian home,
Which received him like a featherless bird in a nest.

It clothed him, girded him with manners, with wisdom,
In the heat it refreshed him with its shade, like
The vinestock readorning its withered branches,
And now a priest, the church took him for her spouse.

Like a lost bird he stretched his two wings
In Palermo and Contessa, both here and there
He sought honor for the Albanians in all his writings.

Like a silkworm he exhausted himself
And wove, embellished and wrote this treasure
To enrich Albania in every possible way.

I Traveled the Earth

I traveled the earth in search of treasures,
Caused all Albania to blush at my sins,
Alas, how this hellish life deceived me,
Promised me honors, gold, and pleasures.

On the verge of seizing that golden trove,
Those vile wooden boards enclosed my worn body. . . .
Around my tomb weep the folk of Contessa,
I beg you, Lord, forgive them their sins.

GIULIO VARIBOBA
1724–1788

Giulio Variboba, known in Albanian as Jul Variboba, is the first
Arbëresh poet of real talent and is regarded by many Albanians as
the first genuine poet in all of Albanian literature. He was born
in San Giorgio Albanese (Mbuzati) in the province of Cosenza to
a family originally from the Mallakastra region of southern Alba-
nia. He studied at the Corsini seminary in San Benedetto Ullano, a
center of learning and training for the Byzantine Greek priesthood.
Even during his studies, Variboba had shown a definite preference
for the Latin (Catholic) rite over the traditional Byzantine Greek rite
in the Arbëresh Church. In later years, this stance made him quite
unpopular with both his parish and with the local church hierarchy
in Rossano, in particular after his direct appeal to the Pope. He was
eventually forced into exile, initially to Campania and Naples. In
1761 he settled in Rome, where he spent the rest of his days.

Despite the turmoil of these years, Variboba must have known
moments of tranquillity, too, for it was soon after his arrival in Rome
that his long lyric poem *The Life of the Virgin Mary* (*Ghiella e Shën
Mëriis Virghiër* [Rome, 1762]) was published, the only Arbëresh book
printed in the eighteenth century. This loosely structured poem of
4,717 lines, written entirely in the dialect of San Giorgio Albanese
and loaded with much Calabrian Italian vocabulary, is devoted to

the life of the Virgin Mary from her birth to the Assumption. From the poet's own life history and his uncompromising and polemic attitude to church rites, one might be led to expect verse of intense spiritual contemplation, yet the work evinces more of a lighthearted, earthy ballad tone, using Variboba's native Calabria as a background for the nativity and transforming the devout characters of the New Testament into hearty eighteenth-century Calabrian peasants. Variboba is unique in early Albanian literature, both in his clear and simple poetic sensitivities and in the variety of his rhythmic expression, though the quality of his verse does vary considerably. The strength of *The Life of the Virgin Mary,* interspersed as it is with folk songs, lies indeed in its realistic and down-to-earth style, often pervaded with humor and naïveté, and in the fresh local color of its imagery.

The Life of the Virgin Mary

O sweet life, O dear Saint Mary,
Come, inspire our newest verses,
As they should be wrought to please you,
Come and join with us and sing them.

We don't know how best to praise you,
Honor you as you're deserving,
For you're blessed and you love us,
This we state, this is sufficient.

What mortal could ever number
All your graces and your grandeur?
None but God can know your merits,
Others' tongues simply can't sing them.

In the teachings of the Scriptures
You, exalted, weren't included,
Sin, that serpent, has devoured,
Consumed us, poor and wretched people.

GIULIO VARIBOBA

Created only for your Lord,
You trampled, left for dead, the devil,
You alone, by your birth, sinless,
Crushed and smashed his head asunder.

Your mother, Saint Anne, and Saint Joachim
Had no sons, but midst their sad tears,
Sighs and fasting, tribulations,
Bore you by the grace of our Lord.

With vows, masses, and much prayer,
With devotion and affliction,
Good Saint Anne, advanced in age,
Conceived you and did give birth to you.

At your birth, both earth and heaven
Celebrated everywhere, and
Joy you gave when you emerged and,
Like the sun, immaculate, shone.

In a temple you retreated
Three years for our Lord's contentment,
You a rose blossom did give him,
To him lent your virgin flower.

For in you, the Lord exulted,
Fell in love, and you he wished well,
Blessed you, sanctified, transformed you,
Body, Church, and soul united.

An angel brought to you a message,
Brought to you a benediction:
"O blessed woman, what's your answer?
Our Lord did choose you for his mother."

You replied: "I am a virgin,
How can virgins become mothers,
Thus your message does not bless me,
As a virgin, you have cursed me."

The angel spoke: "No, for the Lord
Will enter you and do no damage,
Your virginity he'll render
Purer than it was beforehand.

Like a looking glass in sunlight,
Rays can't burn, they'll but it brighten,
Be not worried, don't be fearful,
The Holy Ghost will come and fill you."

"If the flower will truly save me,"
Said the Lady, "I'll be content
With whate'er he says and wishes,
I'm ready now to do his bidding."

With her "yes," the sky did open,
And into her breast Christ entered,
He became a sweet-faced toddler,
Like a doll or a May flower.

The Holy Ghost, so speaks the Gospel,
Set her heart afire, like red coals,
And with blood, supplied as needed,
Was Christ's body thus created.

And so the Babe was born, the heart's lord,
And the heart's son, say the Scriptures,
Thus in our hearts he takes refuge,
Where he can find rest and respite.

GIULIO VARIBOBA

The Song of the Awakening

Awake, son, sleep no longer!
Awake, for you have slept too much,
    Come on, wake up, my darling.
    Arise, for you've been dozing.
A group of shepherds is coming
In a procession to visit you,
    Listen to them dance and sing,
    Causing the earth and sea to ring.
Drones and flutes,
Reeds and pipes,
    Playing in fair harmony,
    Oh, what verse for your refreshment!
Hearken, son, and enjoy it,
Bless them with these hands of yours,
    Look at all the presents they have for you,
    All the herds that they have brought you,
Touch with your palm this little lambkin,
How white it is, like cotton!
    And how soft this pale cheese!
    See, the shepherds fetched it for you.
The kid with these goats
Was carried by that "black-mouthed" fellow,
    And the sheep covered in wool
    Was led by that "woolly legged" chap.
How sweet is this honeycomb,
Nikolla was here and offered it.
    Milëkoci sent some *giuncata,*
    Get up, son, and we'll have it together,
It's a kind of cheese that shepherds eat.
A bird that looks like a lark
    And a wild dove
    And more fresh cheese from Ngjisku.
Up with you, my son, awaken and taste it,
And bless the shepherds.
    Now a group of worshippers has arrived,
    Singing folk ballads,

Look, son, and enjoy them,
Wake up, for you have had your nap.
    Judith is coming with a rooster
    And has struck up a song.
Ephigenia has brought a cap,
A cabbage pie and a kid goat.
    Malita has lugged a capon,
    And her sister has got a peacock.
Five lengths of ribbon
Have been given by the widow Rutiçela.
    Her daughter's brought some chestnuts,
    Chaffinches and some blackbirds.
Rachel's sporting a belt
To tie around your waist.
    Look what Deborah has for you,
    A bread roll and a cake made with grape juice.
A length of embroidery
Was borne by Susana this morning.
    Sunamita has come with difficulty,
    But brings you a fine mantilla.
With great joy Magdalena
Bears for you a scarlet wrap.
    Eve has come, but without vigor,
    And has for you a fair piece of cloth.
Elizabeth has brought a cross,
Her sister a wallet.
    Lia has some diapers
    And Serafina some eggs.
Noemea, the one who shouts,
Has proffered a scarf and a sash,
    And Sorana, as far as she was able,
    Has packed for you a lace shirt.
Three other peasants
Have brought you grapes and a piece of cake.
    A girl who just says "koka"
    Gave you raisins and some peaches.
And Dilusha, who is married,
Has brought a tiara for me.

GIULIO VARIBOBA

Rebeluça, that poor maiden,
Offers you her heart in her hands,
And Belina, who was pious,
Filched some fruit from Acri.
Martha says that the day after tomorrow,
Her mother will give you some cheese.
Look at everything and bless the gifts and their givers,
Awake, son, sleep no longer!

GIROLAMO DE RADA
1814–1903

Girolamo De Rada, known in Albanian as Jeronim De Rada, is not only the best-known writer of Italo-Albanian literature but also the foremost figure of the Albanian nationalist movement in nineteenth-century Italy. Born the son of a parish priest of Greek rite in Macchia Albanese (Maqi), in the mountains of Cosenza, De Rada attended the college of Saint Adrian in San Demetrio Corone. Already imbued with a passion for his Albanian lineage, he began collecting folklore material at an early age. In October 1834, in accordance with his father's wishes, he registered at the Faculty of Law of the University of Naples, but the main focus of his interests remained folklore and literature.

In Naples in 1836, De Rada published the first edition of his best-known Albanian-language poem, *Songs of Milosao,* under the Italian title *Poesie albanesi del secolo XV: Canti di Milosao, figlio del despota di Scutari* (Albanian Poetry from the Fifteenth Century: Songs of Milosao, Son of the Despot of Shkodra). This most popular of his literary works is a long romantic ballad portraying the love of Milosao, a fictitious young nobleman in fifteenth-century Shkodra (Scutari) who has returned home from Thessalonica. There, at the village fountain, he encounters and falls in love with Rina, the daughter of the shepherd Kollogre. De Rada was the harbinger and first audible voice of the romantic movement in Albanian literature, a movement that, inspired by his unfailing energy on behalf of national awakening among Albanians in Italy and in the Balkans, was to evolve into the romantic nationalism characteristic of the Rilindja period in Albania.

The Earth Had Transformed the Oaks

The earth had transformed the oaks,
Fresh seawater sparkled
Blue at the new day rising;
But the dove of Anacreon
Lived on in ancient Tempe.
One day it departed for the mountains for water
And did not return as was its habit.
It did not freeze in the snow
Nor was it wounded by an arrow,
But flew onward until it landed
At my happy home.
When the house and land
Reappeared beside the sea at dawn,
What joy welled in my eyes.
It awoke me, brushing
Against the windowpanes.
I arose and looked outside:
The grapes in the ripening vineyards
Covered our fields,
The blossoming flax
Swayed in the wind,
Gently smiling, and like its blossoms
Was the color of the sky.
You could look out and forget
The cares of this world.
The gleaners were singing
Amidst the sheaves. I had just
Returned from abroad, to be reunited
With my sisters. My name was
Constantly on my mother's lips.
A joy filled my body

GIROLAMO DE RADA

Like that of a fair maiden
Who, in the warmth of her bed at night,
Senses her breasts
Beginning to swell.

Like Two Radiant Lips

The vineyards were golden,
Foxes with their exhausted young
Were descending from the mountains
At the end of the harvest,
At the time of year when the sun
Retreats from such places (as mothers
Who have sung and danced retreat from earth),
At the time I left for Fjokat.
Tall and with embroidered cuffs
And braided hair
Bound in a white ribbon,
There was a maiden at the fountain,
Pensive her brow,
Her scarf tied to a blue sash
Extending to the ground.
The moment she sensed my presence
She turned toward me,
Elegant and graceful,
Trembling with joy.
The lad: "Will you give me a drop of your water, maiden?"
The maid: "As much as you wish, sir."
"Whose daughter are you, maiden?"
"Are you not from here?"
"When as a lad I left home
For Thessalonica, there were no maidens
In the village with such charm."
Lifting her jug
She said blushingly:

"I am the daughter of Kollogre"
And departed, her head uncovered.
Though she took a path,
The thorns that covered it
Did not scratch her,
For I held them back
With my bleeding arms.
We seemed on that evening
Like two radiant lips
In a moment of ecstasy.

Can a Kiss Be Sweeter?

It was Sunday morning
And the son of the noble matron
Went to visit the fair maid
To ask for a drop of water,
For he was dying of thirst.
He found her alone by the hearth
Braiding her hair.
They loved one another, but spoke not of their love,
The maiden with a smile on her lips:
"Why must you fly off like the wind?"
"They're awaiting me for discus throwing."
"Wait a moment, I've kept
Two ripe apples for you."
Holding her combed hair
With one raised hand
Over her pale ears,
She plunged the other into her bodice
And pulled out the apples,
Placing them in his hands,
Blushing with embarrassment.
Tell me, O lovers,
Can a kiss be sweeter?

GIUSEPPE SEREMBE
1844–1901

Italo-Albanian lyric poet Giuseppe Serembe, known in Albanian as Zef Serembe, was born in San Cosmo Albanese (Strigari), in the Calabrian province of Cosenza, and studied at the college of Saint Adrian. At an early age, he fell in love with a girl from his native village who emigrated to Brazil with her family and subsequently died. Obsessed by this loss and by the thought of finding at least her grave, Serembe set sail for Brazil in 1874 in search of a new life. After a brief love affair there, he returned to Europe, disappointed and dejected. In 1893 he traveled to the United States, where he lived for about two years. A volume of his Italian verse was published in New York in 1895. In 1897, he emigrated from his native Calabria to South America a second time and tried to start a new life in Buenos Aires. The following year he fell ill and died in 1901 in São Paulo.

Many of Serembe's works (poetry, drama, and a translation of the Psalms of David), which he constantly altered and revised, were lost in the course of his unsettled existence. Thirty-nine of his Albanian poems were published posthumously in *Verse* (*Vjersha* [Milan, 1926]) by his nephew, Cosmo Serembe. Giuseppe Serembe's verse, despondent and melancholic in character and yet often patriotic and idealistic in inspiration, is considered by many to rank among the best lyric poetry ever produced in Albanian before modern times. His themes range from melodious lyrics on love to eulogies on his native land (be it Italy, land of his birth, or Albania, land of his dreams), elegant poems on friendship and the beauties of nature, and verse of religious inspiration. He was a poet of sentiment, primarily of solitude and disillusionment.

Song of Longing

You are angry with me and I know not why,
O fairest apple of paradise lost,
What have I done in my misery that you leave me thus,
How long shall I be deprived of all my joy?

Oh, how bitter were the days
When I saw delight fade from your eyes
Which had filled this soul with such pride
And struck my heart with passion.

No longer I beheld your forehead
At the window, embroidered with sunbeams,
Nor your rare lips, radiant heavens
Now thickly veiled in cloud.

Near your breast, my heart seethes with fire
And my mind with worry,
No respite do I encounter, no peace do I find,
Maid, you have ruined my life forever.

Friendship

Across the wide sea the swallow did wend
And feathered its nest in much warmer lands,
It wandered in longing, but did not forget,
When the moment arrived, to go back to its home.

Beating its wings in the strong wind it soared
On the journey returning to its former joy,
But a fierce storm arose on the way and did slay it,
Thus in its yearning the swallow passed on.

Such is the destiny of sacred friendship,
Two loving hearts, be they far from each other,
Strive to unite, though divided by fate.

Evil oblivion for them has no power,
And if death should sever the thread of their lives,
A sole thought in tears will bow over the tomb.

GIUSEPPE SEREMBE

■ □ ■ □ ■

RILINDJA AND CLASSICAL
TWENTIETH-CENTURY POETRY

PASHKO VASA
1825–1892

From northern Albania, Pashko Vasa (also known as Wassa Effendi, Vaso Pasha, or Vaso Pasha Shkodrani) played a key role in the Rilindja culture of the nineteenth century. This statesman, poet, novelist, and patriot was born in Shkodra. In 1847, full of ideals and courage, he set off for Italy on the eve of the turbulent events that took place there and elsewhere in Europe in 1848. The following year, as an Ottoman citizen, he was expelled to Constantinople. In Constantinople, he obtained a position at the Ministry of Foreign Affairs, whence he was seconded to London for a time, to the imperial Ottoman embassy to the Court of St. James's. He later served the Sublime Porte in various positions of authority. He acquired the title of pasha and, on July 18, 1883, became governor general of Lebanon, a post reserved by international treaty for a Catholic of Ottoman nationality and a position he apparently held, true to the traditions of Lebanon then and now, in an atmosphere of Levantine corruption and family intrigue. He spent the last years of his life there and died in Beirut after a long illness on June 29, 1892.

Vasa is the author of one poem, the most influential and perhaps the most popular ever written in Albanian, which has ensured him his deserved place in Albanian literary history, the famous "O Albania, Poor Albania." This stirring appeal for a national awakening is thought to have been written in the period between 1878, the dramatic year of the establishment of the League of Prizren, and 1880.

O Albania, Poor Albania

O Albania, poor Albania,
Who has shoved your head in ashes?
Once you were a fine, great lady,
All the world's men called you mother.
Once you had such wealth and goodness,
With fair maidens, strapping young lads,

Herds and land, rich fields and produce,
Flashing guns, Italian weapons,
Heroic fellows and pure women,
You reigned as their best companion.

At rifle's blast, at flash of lightning
The Albanian mastered battle,
Thus he fought and thus he perished,
Leaving ne'er misdeeds behind him.
When an Albanian swore an oath did
All the Balkans tremble at him,
When he charged in savage battle,
Always he returned a victor.

How fare you today, Albania?
Like an oak tree groundward falling!
Trampled now, the world walks o'er you,
No one has a kind word for you.
Like snowcapped peaks, like fields abloom
You were clothed, you're now in tatters,
You've no name or reputation,
In your plight you have destroyed them.

Albanians, you are killing kinfolk,
You're split in a hundred factions,
Some believe in God or Allah,
Say "I'm Turk," or "I am Latin,"
Say "I'm Greek," or "I am Slavic,"
But you're brothers, hapless people!
You've been duped by priests and hodjas
To divide you, keep you wretched,
When the stranger shares your hearthside,
Puts to shame your wife and sister,
You still serve him, gaining little,
You forget your forebears' pledges,
You are serfs to foreign landlords,
Who have not your blood or language!

Weep, lament, O swords and rifles,
The Albanian bird's been snared, imprisoned!
Weep with us, O dauntless heroes,
For Albania's toppled, face-smeared,
Neither bread nor meat remaining,
Fire in hearth, nor light, nor pine torch,
Drained of blood and of friends' honor,
She's defiled and now has fallen!

Gather round now, maids and women,
You with fair eyes know of weeping,
Come and mourn our poor Albania,
She has lost her honor, virtue,
She's a wife without a husband,
She's a mother with no offspring!

Who has the heart to let her perish,
Once a heroine, now so weakened!
Well-loved mother, dare we leave her
To fall under foreign boot heels?

No one wishes such shame on her,
Each of us dreads such misfortune!
Before Albania's thus forsaken
Let our men die, bearing rifles.

Wake, Albanian, from your slumber,
Let us, brothers, swear in common
And not look to church or mosque,
The Albanian's faith is Albanianism!

From Bar down to far Preveza
Shall the sun spread forth its warm rays,
Our forefathers left us this land,
Let none touch it, for we'll all die!
Let us fall as did our forebears
And not shame ourselves before God!

PASHKO VASA

NAIM BEY FRASHËRI
1846–1900

Naim Bey Frashëri is considered by many Albanians to be the national poet of Albania. He spent his childhood in the village of Frashër, where, at a Bektashi monastery, he was imbued with the spiritual traditions of the Orient. His education in Janina (Ioánnina) made of him a prime example of a late nineteenth-century Ottoman intellectual equally at home in both cultures, the Western and the Oriental. Frashëri was the author of a total of twenty-two works: four in Turkish, one in Persian, two in Greek, and fifteen in Albanian. Among his Albanian poetry collections, for which Frashëri is primarily remembered, is the volume *The Flowers of Spring* (*Luletë e verësë* [Bucharest, 1890]), in which he paid tribute to the beauties of the Albanian countryside in twenty-three poems of rich sonority. In the poems, the pantheistic philosophy of his Bektashi upbringing and the strong influence of the Persian classics are coupled harmoniously with patriotic idealism—literary creativity serving the goal of national identity.

The significance of Frashëri as a Rilindja poet and indeed as a national poet rests not so much upon his talents of literary expression nor on the artistic quality of his verse, but rather upon the sociopolitical, philosophical, and religious messages it transmitted, which were aimed above all at national awareness and, in the Bektashi tradition, at overcoming religious barriers within the country. His influence upon Albanian writers at the beginning of the twentieth century was enormous. Many of his poems were set to music during his lifetime and were sung as folk songs. If one compares the state of Albanian literature before and after the arrival of Naim Frashëri, one becomes aware of the major role he played in transforming Albanian into a literary language of substantial refinement.

O Mountains of Albania

O mountains of Albania and you, O trees so lofty,
Broad plains with all your flowers, day and night I contemplate you,

You highlands so exquisite, and you streams and rivers sparkling,
O peaks and promontories, and you slopes, cliffs, verdant forests,
Of the herds and flocks I'll sing out which you hold and which you
    nourish.
O you blessed, sacred places, you inspire and delight me!
    You, Albania, give me honor, and you name me as Albanian,
And my heart you have replenished both with ardor and desire.
    Albania! Oh, my mother! Though in exile I am longing,
My heart has ne'er forgotten all the love you've given to me.
    When a lambkin from its flock strays and does hear its mother's
        bleating,
Once or twice it will give answer and will flee in her direction,
Were others, twenty-, thirtyfold, to block its path and scare it,
Despite its fright it would return, pass through them like an arrow,
Thus my wretched heart in exile, here in foreign land a-pining,
Hastens back unto that country, swift advancing and in yearning.
    Where cold springwater bubbles and cool breezes blow in
        summer,
Where the foliage grows so fairly, where the flowers have such
        fragrance,
Where the shepherd plays his reed pipe to the grazing of the cattle,
Where the goats, their bells resounding, rest, yes 'tis the land I
        long for.

The Words of the Candle

Here among you have I risen,
And aflame am I now blazing,
Just a bit of light to give you,
That I change your night to daytime,
I'll combust and I will wither,
Be consumed and be extinguished,
Just to give you brightness, vision,
That you notice one another,
For you will I fade and tarnish,
Of me there will be no remnant,

NAIM BEY FRASHËRI

I will burn, in tears lamenting,
My desire I cannot suffer.
Of the fire I am not fearful,
I will never be extinguished
If I burn of my desire,
Try to shine as best I'm able.
When you see that I have vanished,
Do not think that I have perished,
I'm alive, among the living,
In the rays of truth I'm standing,
In your souls do I take refuge,
Do not think I'm stranger to you,
Patience was bestowed upon me,
Thus I glow with steadfast courage,
Doing good is all I long for,
That you not remain in darkness.
Forward now and gather round me
Talk, smile, eat, drink, and make merry,
Love within my soul is harbored,
Yes, for mankind am I flaming,
Let me melt and let me smolder,
To grow cold I do not wish for.
Let my wretched corpse be consumed
For our true God the Almighty,
May my lungs scorch, charred to ashes,
For mankind I'll melt and vanish,
With me all man's joys I'll carry,
Bear them to the Lord Almighty.
Humanity is what I long for,
Goodness, gentleness, and wisdom,
If you'll with me be companions,
If you'll love me as I love you,
If you all love one another,
Work not for the Prince of Darkness.
Venture toward me, fleeting heart, do
Come, approach this fire a little!
Though the flame may singe your wings, it's

Sure to sanctify your spirit.
With the torch that here consumes me
I the eyes of men have opened,
Been of them a true companion.
I do know them, they do know me,
I've observed them all in passing,
Mothers, kith and kin, and fathers,
All of them are my concern still,
All who lived here on this planet,
Even now I see them 'mongst you,
For I recognize their spirits.
I, like you, have changed, transfigured,
Changed and altered my companions,
Many times have I turned into
Earth and wind and fire and water.
I'm a spark come from the heavens,
From the sun I'm glowing embers,
Through the skies I fly, a-soaring,
And live deep within the ocean,
Often in the soil I sleep or
Take my rest in fruits and honey,
I'm a suckling lamb or kid goat,
Flower, grass, or leaves a-sprouting,
So much do I have to tell you,
Yet I fear my speech will fail me.
What's the point to put to paper
Words this flickering tongue's inspired?

The Flute

Listen to the flute a-speaking,
Tell the tale of wretched exile,
Weeping for this world of sorrow
Using words of truth to spin it.

NAIM BEY FRASHËRI

Since the day they seized and took me
From my friends and my companions,
Men and women have been weeping
At the echo of my sobbing.

I have rent my breast from beating,
Gaping holes have made within it,
How I've wept and have lamented,
Thousand sighs my heart has rendered.

I'm a friend and blithe companion
Both of this world's happy people
And of all folk sad, embittered,
With them do I make alliance.

Whate'er be the situation,
I can cry and mourn in yearning,
At any time and any place will
My heart sigh and be a-moaning.

All the world does listen to me,
Sees though only my appearance,
Of my wishes they know nothing,
Nor the fire that burns within me.

People come and gather round me
When I weep and tell of longing,
Yet they do not know my secret,
Thus I find no consolation.

Those abandoned, hearts forsaken,
Of the flute become companions,
Some, its mellow scales a-hearing,
Lose their minds, their wits completely.

Human falsehood and illusion!
The flute's voice is not mere wind, it
Has the fire of love within it
When that lowly reed is fingered.

When it plays, the heavens brighten,
When it plays, do hearts take courage,
When it plays, the summer blossoms,
When it plays, the soul's ecstatic.

To the rose it lends its fragrance,
And to beauty adds an aura,
Gives the nightingale its music,
Charm bestows upon the cosmos.

Of that fire to the heavens
Rising, flickering and flaming,
Does it make the sun and stars which
God within his hands is holding.

From that fire, true God Almighty
All the firmament he fashioned,
Sent the spark of life, creating
Humankind after his likeness.

Fire, O blessed fire a-blazing,
I with you have been united,
Thus am purified and blended.
Never leave me, my beloved!

ANDON ZAKO ÇAJUPI
1866–1930

Andon Zako Çajupi was born in Sheper, a village in the upper Zago-
ria region of southern Albania, as the son of a rich tobacco merchant,
Harito Çako, who did business in Kavála and Egypt. The young

Andon Zako, who usually preferred this spelling of his surname and later adopted the pseudonym Çajupi, emigrated, in 1882, to Egypt, where he studied for five years at the French lycée in Alexandria. In 1887, he went on to study law at the University of Geneva. Back in Egypt, Çajupi apprenticed for three years with a German law firm in Cairo. His legal career came to a swift conclusion when he made the strategic mistake of defending a French company in a dispute against the interests of the khedive. Financially independent, however, Çajupi bore this professional calamity with ease. He withdrew to his villa in Heliopolis, near Cairo, and devoted himself subsequently to literature and to the consolidation of the thriving Albanian nationalist movement in Egypt.

The most significant phase of Çajupi's literary and nationalist activities was from 1898 to 1912. In 1902 he published the poetry volume for which he is best remembered: *Father Tomorr (Baba-Tomorri* [Cairo]). This collection, named after Mount Tomorr in central Albania, the Parnassus of Albanian mythology, contains light verse on mostly nationalist themes. The work was an immediate success. Indeed, no volume of Albanian poetry had proven so popular among Albanians at home and abroad since the collections of Naim Frashëri. Though there are many technical imperfections in his poems, their straightforward octosyllabic rhythms reminiscent of southern Albanian folk songs, their unequivocal messages, and their patriotic inspiration made them extremely popular with both adults and children.

My Village

The mountains rich in stone,
The meadows full of grass,
The fields replete with wheat,
Beyond them is a river.

Across from it the village
With church and rows of gravestones,
And standing all around it
Are humble, tiny houses.

Frigid is the water,
The wind blows, but no matter,
The nightingale proclaims it:
Gazelle-like are the women.

Lying in the shade, men
Playing, busy chatting,
Misfortune cannot strike them,
For they're living off their women.

Women in the fields, and
In the vineyards, women,
Women harvest hay, all
Day and night a-toiling.

Women do the threshing,
Reap the harvest, women,
Leaving before sunrise,
After dark returning!

For their husbands, women
Scorch out in the sunshine,
Working, never resting—
Not even on a Sunday!

Poor Albanian woman,
All the time a-slaving,
And when homeward's wended,
Makes both lunch and supper.

What about your husband
Lounging by the fountain?
O my wretched woman,
You run, too, the household!

Motherland

Motherland's the country
Where I first raised my head,
Where I loved my parents,
Where every stone knows me,
Where I made my home,
Where I first knew God,
Where my ancestors lived,
And left their graves behind them,
Where I grew on bits of bread,
Where I learned to speak my language,
Where I have my friends and family,
Where I've laughed and where I've cried,
Where I dwell with mirth and hope,
Where I one day long to perish.

Servitude

Dear motherland of mine,
I love you as you are,
But if I saw you free,
I'd love you even more.

Weep, O forests, plains, and stones,
Weep, O mountains under snows,
Poor Albania is abandoned,
Never will she see the light,

Veiled forever is the country
In a thick and somber blight.

Darkness and misfortune on us,
Thunder, lightning all around us,
Do we live with hearts a-frozen,
Dwell in fear, deprived of joy,
None in song do raise their voices,
And the nightingales are grieving.

What disaster, desolation!
In their nests the birds take shelter,
Yet the people flee their own soil,
For a savage law does rule it,
Yes, Albania, we yearn for you,
Refugees in states so foreign.

How can you endure such serfdom,
O Albania, wretched country?
You've saved other nations while you
Bear this heavy yoke and burden.
O Albanians, swear an oath that
You will now fight for your homeland.

Dear motherland of mine,
I love you as you are,
But if I saw you free,
I'd love you even more.

NDRE MJEDA
1866–1937

Classical poet Ndre Mjeda bridges the gap between late nineteenth-
century Rilindja culture and the dynamic literary creativity of the
independence period. Mjeda was born in Shkodra and, like so

many other Gheg writers of the period, was educated by the Jesuits. The Society of Jesus sent the young man abroad for studies and training. From 1887 to 1891, he taught music at the College of Marco Girolamo Vida in Cremona, on the Po River, and later studied for a couple of years at the theological faculty of a Gregorian college in Kraków in Catholic Poland. Mjeda was a member of the Literary Commission, set up in Shkodra on September 1, 1916, under the Austro-Hungarian administration, and, from 1920 to 1924, he served as a deputy in the National Assembly. After the defeat of Fan Noli's June Revolution and the definitive rise of the Zogu dictatorship at the end of 1924, he withdrew from politics and taught Albanian language and literature at the Jesuit college in Shkodra, where he died. Mjeda's poetry, in particular his collection *Juvenilia* (Vienna, 1917), is noted for its classical style and for its purity of language. Though not covering an especially wide range of themes, his verse evinces a particularly refined language, under the influence of the nineteenth-century Italian classics, and, in general, a high level of metric finesse.

Winter

O'er fields and o'er mountains
Blows the bitter polar blast,
O north wind, halt your fury,
And you, frost, don't freeze me over,
Don't congeal these last drops of blood,
Cringe and cower, poor old man.

With scythe in hand, winter has come,
Has culled the leaves and cropped the grass.
Snow whirls o'er the balcony.
The piteous elder, feeble and frigid,
In failing voice repeats:
"Cringe and cower, poor old man."

To the Albanian Eagle

High amongst the clouds, above the cliffs
Sparkling in perennial snow,
Like lightning, like an arrow,
Soars on sibilant wings
Midst the peaks and jagged rocks
The eagle in the first rays of dawn.

The azure sky above its head,
Companion of the stars, glows
Like jewels, like the shimmering
Gold of a bridal gown,
Or the radiant night in which
A god bestows wisdom and grace.

Your kingdom is silent,
Eagle, arbiter of freedom,
And in the empty wastes
The harmony of stars
And the rising moon give you comfort,
And the pensive Muse is heard.

But above the forlorn flatland
Where your children in keening lie,
Thunder resounds,
Lightning flashes,
And you above those peaks
Hear no echo of their lament.

O descend to us, royal
Eagle, once more, as you did
When in battle, majestic
Castrioti the Great shone forth
And the whole world trembled
At the menace of his sword.

NDRE MJEDA

Freedom

I

Tell me, eagles, birds of the highlands,
Do the rays of freedom shine upon those peaks,
In the rugged mountain pastures and clearings
Where springs of fresh water murmur in longing?

Have you heard the echo of its anthem
On your flights o'er the cliffs,
Have you heard its comforting song?
Tell me, eagles, birds of the highlands.

"Freedom, freedom," the mountains cry,
But can we find it on the earth we ply,
Or will slavery veil our every step?

Fly, eagle, fly to horizons far away,
The mountains surrounding Albania, survey,
Tell us where freedom takes its source.

. . . .

V

Freedom is yours! We have iron bars,
Yet we languish in the mists and somber night,
No one knows our name, stripped of our country,
We are slaves of the strangers on our own soil.

Like chattel sold to the butcher, we're driven,
Crazed, by his cane where we don't wish to go,
Sighs and lamentation on the lips of our people,
Suffering and grief is the name of our land.

The storm of highland heroes in vain
Infiltrates the sleeping plain
Like a bolt of lightning from the clouds.

Crushed by cruel oppression and travail,
Shake in their tombs to no avail
The forgotten bones of Dukagjini and Skanderbeg the Hero.

VI

But no, the Albanian race has not been stamped out,
Wearied by the beatings of a harsh enemy,
Bowed by the darkness of servitude,
It broods and waits for its sudden awakening.

And behold, the flashing strokes of freedom
Extend through the mountains, in stealth advance
From hut to hut, yes, the shadow of Skanderbeg,
A new spirit expands throughout the land.

The mothers of Hoti tend cradles, childbed,
Where fledgling young heroes are nurtured and fed
On the milk of revolt.
And high in the mountains, splendor regal,
Claws outstretched, the Albanian eagle
Spreads its formidable wings.

GJERGJ FISHTA
1871–1940

By far the greatest and most influential figure of Albanian literature
in the first half of the twentieth century was the Franciscan pater
Gjergj Fishta, who, more than any other writer, gave artistic expres-
sion to the searching soul of the now sovereign Albanian nation.
Lauded and celebrated until World War II as the national poet of
Albania and the Albanian Homer, Fishta fell into sudden oblivion
when the Communists took power in November 1944. Mere men-
tion of his name became taboo for forty-six years.

Fishta's name is indelibly linked to one great work, indeed to one
of the most astounding creations in all the history of Albanian litera-

ture, *The Highland Lute* (*Lahuta e malcís* [Shkodra, 1937]). *The Highland Lute* is a 15,613-line historical verse epic focusing on the Albanian struggle for independence. It constitutes a panorama of northern Albanian history from 1858 to 1913. This literary masterpiece was composed primarily between 1902 and 1909, though it was refined and amended by its author over a thirty-year period. It constitutes the first Albanian-language contribution to world literature. *The Highland Lute* was first published in its entirety in English in 2005.

Mehmet Ali Pasha

In the *vilayet* wires were humming:
"All ye *bayraktars* and chieftains,
All the beys and noble rulers
From Kaçanik to Qafa e Diellit
Hasten forthwith to Gjakova.
A new pasha's been appointed
Who will speak words of importance
To the chieftains of Albania
At Abdullah Dreni's mansion."
After three days, three nights, gathered
All the chieftains in Gjakova,
Some were beys and others *agas,*
Bayraktars and *voyvodes* met there.
As their leaders, came two nobles,
Ali Pasha and Haxhi Zeka,
Both of them by pledge united,
Like two bullets in a flintlock.
To the pasha did they hasten,
Were received well by the pasha,
Well by Mehmet Ali and he
Served them coffee and tobacco,
Of their kith and kin inquiring,
Of their commerce and their produce,
Of their clerks and their assistants,
And how they in life were faring,

If they had enough to live on.
Then he turned to them, expounding:
"Greetings from our father sultan,
You're the flowers in his vase here,
Like an amulet he holds you
Under arm, you're like a treasure,
Like eyes below eyebrows guarded.
Now have come hard times upon us
For the kings and for the sultan,
All the more since Prince Nikolla
Sees no way out of his anguish,
Lost up in Cetinje's crags and
But a pipe to call his own there.
Rocks and trees feel pity for him.
Therefore did the kings take counsel,
They've reflected and decided
That he beg of Stamboul's sultan,
Plead to get a piece of wasteland,
Just a field down near Albania,
Just enough to keep him going,
For, by God, he's in dire straits now.
And the sultan, long life to him,
Was informed of their decision
And accorded Montenegro:
Hoti, Gruda, Plava, Gucia . . . "
"Oh, my God, he's made an error,"
Sputtered Ali Pasha, angry,
"Never will this venture prosper,
Albania's not some coin for beggars,
To be passed out to the kings there.
Our land, unlike other countries,
Was not conquered by the sultan,
Like some other Balkan nations.
Partner to us is the sultan,
One who's bound by faith and *besa*,
Sworn to recognize Albania,
To respect our ancient Kanun,
And not interfere with customs.

GJERGJ FISHTA

95

We have promised to fight for him
Should a foe make war, invading.
We've for our part kept our promise.
We made ready when he called us,
And in Yemen waged war for him,
And in Greece did we do battle,
Fought the Slavs and the Armenians,
For ourselves did we take nothing,
Nothing gained and no advantage.
Leaving house and home defenseless,
Thieves and robbers on our carpets.
In a noose hung those not guilty,
Infidels did steal our cattle,
Two cents' worth was manly honor,
One cigar a man's head severed.
Now it seems our father sultan
Wants to give away our country
Like a fig within a basket,
And to whom? To Montenegro!
Listen, pasha of the sultan,
Take your knapsack back to Stamboul,
This our land's a vicious country,
Thorns will wound you on the byways,
And, as to our nation's borders,
They were years ago established,
Marked by an Albanian saber,
And that prince of Montenegro
He'll, God help me, not extract it
Even with the might of boar tusks."
   What retorted then the pasha?
"Look, Albanian, have you gone mad,
Lost to faith and to the imam?
Turks do not speak in this manner.
Who're these partners of the sultan?
Pair of thieves and mountain bandits
To be caught and to be strung up,
Hogs for casting in the pigsty?
Were it not for Stamboul's sultan,

There would be no sunlight shining,
Would no kings on earth be living.
You claim you're the sultan's partners,
You Albanian mountain bandits.
There is no Albanian people,
Only Allah, sultan, Turkey!"
Then the watchmen's captain entered,
Seized, lined up the men before him,
Like a herd kept by a shepherd
When returning home at sunset,
Locked them in the horses' stable,
All the chieftains of Albania.

A vile deed was thus committed.
Not for true men cane and prison,
Better for them noose or saber.
A gross act when perpetrated
Only serves to breed more evil,
Flowing brooks become a torrent.
Thus the pasha made an error
Taking prisoner all the chieftains.
Earth did not explode with fury,
Spewing them back to the surface,
No one rushed to their assistance,
But they have their households, servants,
But they have their tribes and brothers.
Tribes and households will make clear that
They this evil will not suffer.
Thus will Mehmet Ali Pasha
One day face a great dilemma,
Shake his head between his two hands
For his crime against the chieftains.

That the pasha's in a tight spot
Is perhaps not so important.
I Abdullah Dreni pity,
Him, who's been host to a viper,
For the pasha is his guest there,
Spending day and nighttime with him,
With his repasts takes refreshment,

Roasts of meat for lunch and supper,
Mincemeat pastry every mealtime,
Feasts in bounty to his kneecaps,
True Albanian reception.
Yes, I fear Abdullah Dreni
May himself be in a tight spot
From the guest that he's admitted.
For myself, I can't imagine
High Albania will not rally,
Will not move, the northern highlands,
Will not act to free their leaders,
So that, too, the sultan's pasha
Comprehends the act committed
When he seized Albania's chieftains.
What of poor Abdullah Dreni?
Every guest must be protected.
He'll not put to shame Gjakova,
He who's skilled in firing rifles.
Thus I fear, it won't be long 'til
There'll be shooting in Gjakova.
For a war cry has been sounded
From Kaçanik to Qafa e Diellit,
Calling Sharri, Boletini,
Every hearth must send a man off
With his weapons to Gjakova.
Thither pushed Peja, Kosova,
Thither rushed Reka, Rogova,
Up in arms Gashi, Krasniqi,
Joined by Plava and Gucia,
To Gjakova's plain they swarmed up
Like an anthill by a tree trunk.
    Lo, our foes deride us, saying,
"Ne'er together work Albanians!"
Touch, though, their forefathers' country,
Dare infringe upon their honor,
They will congregate, will show you
That they're able to join forces,
Set upon their foe, united,

Like the wolves of Kaçanik when
Hunger strikes them in December.
Thus the pasha, Mehmet Pasha,
Had in Stamboul to himself thought
They would never reach agreement,
Now with his own eyes he's witnessed
All that manly youth a-blossom
On the hillsides of Gjakova.
Head in hands he's now regretted
What he's done, the act committed
'gainst the chieftains of Albania.

Mehmet asked Abdullah Dreni:
"Why have all these people gathered,
Are they members of a wedding,
Are they conscripts of the sultan
Setting off to join the army?"

"Long life to you," bade Abdullah,
"They're no members of a wedding,
They're no conscripts of the sultan
Setting off to join the army.
No, they're lads from High Albania,
Here to talk to you, assembled,
Men that sent to you their chieftains,
Who did not return, are missing."

Hearing, scowled the pasha at him,
For he'd never dared imagine
That so many men would muster
To defend their cause and interests.
To the captain of the guards said:
"Quickly free Albania's chieftains,
They've been pardoned by the sultan,"
And the chieftains, freed, departed,
Asking not to meet the pasha.
To Gjakova's plain they hastened,
There united all the people,
And began to talk, discussing,
What to do in such a matter,
Being sold out by the sultan,

GJERGJ FISHTA

Being sold to Montenegro,
Sold out for a tray of shortcake,
For this pasha, Mehmet Pasha,
Who to them was sent from Stamboul
Had bestowed upon the prince their
Hoti, Gruda, Plava, Gucia.
All those present cried: "Our homeland
We will not abandon living,
As we are, we'd rather perish
Than be in the prince's clutches.
And that pasha sent from Stamboul,
Let us keep him here and judge him,
So that kings and sultan learn to
Keep their hands off of our country!"
    To his feet rose Haxhi Zeka,
Stood up and addressed the people:
"Noble is the house of Dreni
Where the blind and lame are welcome,
And Abdullah Bey's a hero,
So we'll send a message, asking
If he'll give to us the pasha,
Or if he insists on guest's rights."
Wise man is this Haxhi Zeka,
Wise men always speak with reason,
Guests cannot be handed over,
Be they strangers or Albanians,
Or the host will be dishonored.
    To the bey's door went the herald,
To Abdullah Bey explaining:
"O Abdullah Bey, we greet you,
Salutations from the people,
Tell us, will you hand the scoundrel
Hiding in your home out to us?
We've a bone to pick now with him."
    To him turned the bey, replying:
"I don't know and cannot tell you,
Cannot judge if he's a scoundrel,
For, alas, I did not quiz him,

That's not what my father taught me,
I'm not wont to ask my guests here
Who they are or what's their business,
Where they're going, where they've come from,
What their work is, what their wages.
Father taught me one thing only:
'Don't betray your guests, no, never!'
If the people should demand it,
I will give them all I'm heir to,
I will give up highlands, lowlands,
I will give fields plowed and fallow,
I will give up land and houses,
I will give them barns and fodder,
I will give them herds and sheepfolds,
Goats and sheep will I give to them,
But my guests and honor never!"
    They received the message from him.
Bey and guests were in the tower
Watched by fifty Fani tribesmen,
Men whose teeth could bite through iron,
Of them Oshi, son of Nuro,
Three hearts in him, what a hero,
Eyes like lightning, he'd not suffer
That a pasha break the Kanun,
That a bey destroy a village,
That an *aga* steal the food stocks.
    What said Hoxha Korenica:
"Listen Oshi, son of Nuro,
You're from Fani, man of reason,
You know what the law requires.
Go and tell Abdullah Dreni
To hand out the sultan's pasha.
Let us have that scoundrel Mehmet,
For the Kanun of the mountains
Does not cover guests if hostile."
    Oshi spoke from the embrasure:
"By my faith, Hoxha Effendi,
Me the bey has not assigned to

Talk of laws or to take captives,
We've no custom in this country
To hand out our guests on order,
Only by gunpowder, rifles.
I have learned that it's not seemly
For a host to give his guest up.
We'll forgive a family murder,
Yield to insult or a beating,
But we'll not betray a guest who
Bread and salt has eaten with us.
He's no meat sold by a butcher,
Dullo Dreni will not do it.
He will go through fire and water,
But he'll hand his guest to no one.
Proof of it's my *huta* flintlock."
And a shot rang from the *huta*.

   Praise be to our God Almighty,
For the shot from Oshi's *huta*
O'er Çabrati Hill did ring out,
All of Gramoleci shuddered,
Raged the battle, weapons blazing,
As the men slew one another,
Killed Albanians one another
For a pasha of the sultan,
May God curse him and confound him!
All the foreigners who've come here
Always augured evil for us,
For our poor Albanian homeland.
Like a doom-portending raven,
Can you see the dark clouds chafing,
Here to rain upon Gjakova,
All because of that one stranger
Who has brought but evil with him?
Mired in war are the Albanians,
Firing arms at one another,
Some to kill the sultan's pasha,
Some to save the sultan's pasha,
"He's my guest," says someone shouting,

"He's my foe," screams out another.
Smashing one another's skulls in,
Squashing them like gherkins, pumpkins
Sold in Vraka at the market,
Should have sworn their faith and *besa,*
Should have fought the Turks and *shkjas* who've
Left our homeland weakened, withered,
We are killing one another.
Sad it is to see a guest slain,
Sad to see a herald slaughtered,
Of no crime the herald's guilty.
Worst of all's to kill your brother.
Therefore it's a real disaster
That our men are here entangled,
Caught up fighting one another
For a pasha of the sultan,
For a pasha who's a stranger,
Who has brought such evil with him.
So much blood's been spilled now, truly,
Men are cut down in the alleys,
In the lanes, and on verandas,
Not to mention Oshi Nuro
At the embrasure in the tower,
Men, one hundred in their number,
By his hands did fall and perish,
Just to save a Turkish pasha,
Who's perchance some vagrant nomad.
    Full three days and nights the battle,
Rifles ripping through the city,
'til at last, the tower taken,
Slaughtered was the Turkish pasha,
Slain while hiding in the pantry.
For the pasha I've no pity,
No compassion, will not mourn him,
Had they slain two, all the better,
But I mourn Abdullah Dreni,
Shaqir Curri and Ram Rrustemi,
And for Oshi, son of Nuro,

GJERGJ FISHTA

103
▾

Who to save his guest did perish,
As our nation's custom has it.
   Thereupon the people gathered,
Sent a message to the sultan:
"Listen to us, father sultan,
Listen to Kosova's people,
Send Albania a new pasha,
Who will punish evildoers,
Who will pave roads for the travelers,
Who will open mosques and churches
For the Muslims and the Christians.
Such a pasha you can grant us,
For we're in your hands, your subjects,
But don't parcel out Albania
As a present for Nikolla.
God be witness, father sultan,
Do not send us such a pasha
For he's certain to be slaughtered,
As we slaughtered Mehmet Ali,
'Harm no herald,' says the Kanun,
But, because we cannot nab you,
We will slay your emissaries
If they ever try to sell us
Or bestow us on a stranger."
   When the kings had heard the news of
What had happened in Gjakova,
Did they marvel at this people,
Who's this folk and who's this nation,
But a handful, poor and wanting,
(We do not know where they come from,
Nor their name have we heard spoken)
Who've ignored a royal order
And the word of Stamboul's sultan?

Bec Patani Meets His Blood Brother in Battle

   Look, there's Bec Patani nearing,
Broad his brow, as wide as war grounds,
Eyebrows black as raven feathers,
Eyes that flash like rifle powder,
Strike like lightning in the heavens.
Upward did he wind his whiskers,
Body rising like a ramrod,
Fingers straight as a gun barrel,
Dressed, and girded were his weapons,
Wily hero, born a *drangue*
Set to vanquish a *kulshedra.*
Host to strangers, friend to comrades,
Always did he keep his promise,
God bestowed on him these features,
Like of ancient times a hero,
Proud son of George Castrioti.
He caught sight of Milo Spasi,
Coming on that slope toward them
To attack the highland fighters,
Brandishing in hand his saber,
But like during sleet and snowstorms,
He could hardly recognize him,
Only saw a *shkja* was nearing.
In pursuit of him, the fighter
Followed over trails and boulders,
'til he reached that riverbed where
Mil, the living sword, was waiting,
In his hand a saber hoisted,
There to fight Rrushman Hasani,
Stood there stiffly, pallid-faced he,
Steeled and poised for lethal combat.
Bec then peered and recognized him,
Held his pace all of a sudden—
They had been friends and *kumaras*
Having drunk each other's blood two

GJERGJ FISHTA

Years before in Montenegro . . .
. . . .

   "Do my eyes deceive me, brother?
Are you really Milo Spasi?
Never would I have imagined
That I'd meet you in this place here
Where we're fighting one another
Like the wild beasts in the thickets,"
Bec Patani stood there asking.
"Yes, it's me, Bec, that you see, I'm
Milo Spasi, your blood brother,"
Saying, did the fighter sheathe his
Saber which with blood was dripping.
Bec approached him, they embraced
With head to head in highland manner.
"How are you and how've you been there?
How the herds and how your household?"
Bec inquired kindly, saying.
"All alive and well, consid'ring,"
Milo then to him responded,
Grown to one his bushy eyebrows.
"What good fortune that I find you
Here before me now, for ages
Have I yearned for you as were you,
Yes, three hundred times my brother!"
   Has it ever happened that you've
Seen a hound when it's unchained, and
Lunges at a guest approaching
Soon as it espies him and would
Almost tear him into pieces?
Should the owner now, however,
Come out first as host, *kumara,*
Take him home and make him welcome,
Will its rage and anger vanish,
Will its frenzied circling cease and
Slightly with its tail a-wagging,
Will it slowly near the guest and
Take a sniff or two around him.

Soon the hound will lead them home as
If it were a little puppy.
Thus, Rrushman Hasani acted
When he saw him, Bec Patani,
Cheek to cheek with Milo Spasi,
As prescribes the highland Kanun.
In his tracks did stop the fighter,
Stop there with his whiskers drooping,
Curving, curling low before him,
Right down to his belt cascading,
O'er his shoulder was his *huta,*
Blood was flowing down his arms and
Fire was in his ox eyes blazing.
In its sheath he placed his saber,
Then the fighter came advancing,
Shook the hand of Milo Spasi,
"How are you?" he asked of Milo
In amazement, "Hope you've been well."
"How've you been yourself?" the *shkja* asked
Hesitating and embarrassed.
Bec then spoke up: "Listen, Rrushi,
This man here is my blood brother,
Milo Spasi from Rahova,
Who is skilled at war and speaking,
Many Turks and Moors he's slaughtered,
Pared them all like cukes and pumpkins.
All who go to Montenegro,
Slavs, Albanians, be they Christians,
He has helped them, lent assistance,
Proffered bread and salt, protection.
Çul and I, when we in Lezha
Shot and killed that Ali Qorri,
Making foe thus of the sultan,
Fled and made for Montenegro,
Went and were received in honor,
Full three years did we sojourn with
Bread and meat, with wine and raki." . . .
. . . .

GJERGJ FISHTA

107
▾

From the pocket in his mantle
Rrushi pulled out his tobacco,
Rolled for each a cigarette which
Bec then lit up with a flint stone.
Rrushi said to Milo Spasi:
"God has given me a son who's
Three years old at home and growing.
Should it be the will of God and
Should our heads stay on our shoulders
In the midst of all this clamor,
I would have you come to Shkreli,
Come and cut his hair the first time,
I would have you be *kumara*."
    "That is just what I was thinking,"
Said the fellow from Rahova,
Wresting from his belt a pistol,
Pistol made in Montenegro,
With five bullets, nowhere is a
Rifle stronger; and to Rrushman
Did he pass it with the barrel.
Rrushi with a pipe of silver
Ornamented did requite it,
With an oval piece of amber,
Finely wrought with serpent motif
Winding all along it, tooled by
Tuke Jakova, famous goldsmith,
Worth a purse, five hundred pieces.
Then he turned to Bec, commanding:
"Listen, take your friend now with you,
Take him down beyond our trenches,
He'll be safe there. Farewell to you!"
Then the fellows separated,
Bec and Milo to Sutjeska,
Rrushman moved off up the meadows,
Eyes aglow like red-hot embers.

The Mountain Nymphs Mourn the Death of Tringa

Perched atop a boulder's tip
Upon Trojani's mountain pastures
Sat a white *ora* observing
With her sisters all the fighting,
All the warfare down in Nokshiq,
Heard the shrieking and the moaning,
Heard the *oras* and the *zanas*
On Vizitor's mountain meadows.
Hearing, did she understand that
Maybe Vizitor's Great *Zana*,
Slender figure, raised in orchards,
And her flaxen-haired sprite sisters,
May the Lord increase their dance, had
Happened on a fateful pathway.
Thus she said to her companions:
"Listen, sisters, do I beg you,
All that shrieking and that moaning
Which is spewing from Vizitor
Does not sound like jubilation,
Rather seems a sign of sorrow,
Grief and somber lamentation.
It might be a good idea
That we hasten to Vizitor,
That we find out what has happened,
And how fare our distant sisters."
Thus the Good Ones, may God bless them,
Soared into the air together,
Beating golden wings and gliding,
Flew to Vizitor's high pastures.
In a flash the gilded feathers
Fluttered to that mountain venue,
Like some eagles, flexed their clutches,
When they, searching from the heavens,
Zoom past thickets and o'er clearings,
Down to pluck their prey, the victims.
Thus the Earthly Beauties hovered,

GJERGJ FISHTA

Circled Vizitor's high pastures,
Scanning with their eyes to see if
They could spy the *oras, zanas.*
There, the eyes of the Great *Ora*
Focused on a meadow, where the
Fairies, all the *shtozovalles,*
Stood on Vizitor's great pasture
In a circle, there surrounding
Tringa's body. Cheeks a-scratching,
Hair a-tearing, the Great *Zana*
Patted Tringa's face so gently,
Sobbed and moaned, to tears she melted.
Arrow-like, the Earthly Beauties
To that pasture plunged and landed,
Brought a breeze with wings a-beating,
When descending from their journey,
They caused beech-tree leaves to quiver.
When they lit upon that meadow,
Did they see the *zanas* weeping,
Saw them sobbing, cheeks a-scratching,
Saw bent over, the Great *Zana,*
Over Tringa, gently stroking.
How the Good Ones there were staggered,
How they grieved and how lamented,
Down their faces tears were streaming.
    The Great *Ora* of Trojani
Reigned like first rays in the morning,
And a star shone on her forehead,
Down her back did flow and tumble
Locks of silken hair, all wavy,
Flowing were her snow-white garments,
From her flight on high they fluttered,
Shining like the sun at noonday,
'Neath her breasts a golden waistband,
On her feet were gilded sandals,
Like a full moon in the heavens
On a summer evening glowing.
Silver did her forehead shimmer

Over eyebrows, as a mountain
Over pathways shines in splendor
Midst the stars up in the cosmos.
Thus majestic stood the Good One
On the meadow strewn with flowers,
Treading lightly, steps well measured,
Skirting petals of the lilies,
That she not tread on the blossoms,
Roundabout did she proceed and
Make her way to the Great *Zana*,
Placed her arms under her shoulders,
Pulled her to her feet, and with her
Left arm, creamy-hued like ivory,
Wrapped around her thighs fresh lilies.
Tightly did she hold the *zana*,
Pressed her to her breast so gently.
With the other hand, the Beauty
Dressed her hair o'er brow and temples,
With great care did she arrange it
In a kerchief, then said to her,
While the tears her cheeks were drenching:
"Come, good sister, be now stoic,
You are such a valiant woman,
For you're thus, and God's my witness,
Only doing yourself damage.
Come now, be steadfast, my sister,
It will be your death, this weeping."
    The Great *Zana*, head now leaning
In the white arms of her sister,
Sobbing, whining in affliction,
Broken words used as an answer:
"Such misfortune's struck me, sister,
That I've nothing more to live for,
For they've slain my dearest Tringa,
Withered her in youth and blossom,
Both my eyes have now been blinded,
Burnt to ashes all my pastures,
Poisoned are the creeks and torrents.

GJERGJ FISHTA

III
▾

I can no more join the dancing,
Never will I bathe in fountains,
I've no need of shady places,
I've no need of fresh springwater,
No need to pluck lilies, roses,
Chase the butterflies o'er meadows,
Follow ladybirds and glowworms,
Or to nightingales' songs hearken.
May these pleasures ever vanish,
May there be no singing, dancing,
May there ne'er return more springtimes,
Now that wretched Tringa's slaughtered,
Whom above all else I longed for,
May a bolt of lightning fell me."

ASDRENI
1872–1947

Asdreni, pseudonym of Aleks Stavre Drenova, was born in the village of Drenova, about five kilometers from Korça, in southeastern Albania. When he was thirteen, he was sent to Bucharest to join his two elder brothers. It was there in the culturally active Albanian colony that he first came into contact with the ideas and ideals of the nationalist movement in exile. In 1905, he taught at an Albanian school in the port city of Constanza and in the following years became an active figure in the Albanian national movement in Romania. He made a visit to Albania in November 1937 on the twenty-fifth anniversary of independence, hoping after many years of service to the Albanian state to receive a government pension, but to no avail, and died in poverty.

Asdreni began writing poetry and publishing articles in the local press in the early years of the twentieth century. In 1904, he published his first volume of poems, *Sunbeams* (*Rézé djélli* [Bucharest, 1904]), a collection of ninety-nine pieces he dedicated to the Albanian national hero Skanderbeg. Asdreni's second volume, *Dreams and Tears* (*Endra e lote* [Bucharest, 1912]), displayed much greater maturity. The improvement in form, style, and technique and the broadening of the range of themes and ideas are even more evident in his third volume of verse, *Psalms of a Monk* (*Psallme murgu* [Bucharest, 1930]), which marks the zenith of his poetic creativity. Many consider the classically refined *Psalms of a Monk* to be one of the best volumes of Albanian verse published in the twentieth century.

To the Adriatic

I have beheld you, Adriatic, I have beheld you,
A nymph from the twinkling heavens
Sparkling with pearls, your breasts
Heaving gracefully like a sylph's.

I knelt before you as before a goddess,
An apparition of untold beauty.
The rapture I felt, I could not endure,
And departed, tears streaming down my cheeks.

Like molten gold you shimmer,
A fabled palace full of magic,
You sway like maidens in the meadow.

Of youthful grace is your rise and fall,
Sweet memories, a world of wonder
Like a vision of divinity itself.

Forgotten Memories

Where can I find you, O companions of my youth,
That I might once more enjoy that beloved time,
Moments which filled us with such delight
When we played and frolicked in mirth sublime?

Not a drop of sorrow did we feel in our souls,
Our hearts were so fully transfixed by the spring,
Little did we know that our lives would be sad,
And lost youth would nevermore joy to us bring.

Like the autumn leaves which the wind doth chase
Like a fleeting moment of glee which escapes,
Or a summer night's dream that veils its trace,

You can sense, you can see how our elusive hopes
Brought surprising delights to us now and again,
Like the moon's faint rays glimm'ring on a parched plain!

The Oracle of Dodona

In the somber woods of ancient Dodona
Was a Dorian temple by expert hand built,
No other in this world could e'er match its beauty,
Surrounded by statues of silver and gilt.

Laden with gifts appeared kings from afar
To honor the priestess, her speeches divining,
Like hermits they huddled in fasting and prayer
Awaiting their fate, outside they were pining.

But luck and the future possess eyes unbound,
And lots when cast can quickly turn round,
A word is enough, if sent from the heavens. . . .

How many thrones have been toppled and tossed,
And how many leaders' minds have been lost
For failing to heed that old woman's replies?

The Flute

O flute, I worship you with faith and longing
For I was raised, the consort of your trill divine
   from the time I was a lad,
You poured dew into my soul,
At the height of my joy, my feelings merged
   in a tenderness rare.

With you I felt an unslaked sense
Of love for Albanian soil
   Which remains day after day in my dreams,
When your sounds, the treasures of the past,
Traverse my mind like a summer's breeze
   And with deep ecstasy.

When you speak to me and fill me,
Unending voices echo and swell
   In waves like a chorus of angels,
Companions of the peaks, streams, and hills,
From your lips flit fairies
   As if from some majestic palace.

Like starlight and moonbeams in longing,
Sparkling on the surface of the lake,
   I quiver like a lover,
As your words, harbingers of a message
From the Earthly Beauty, with fair tones
   offer us a breath of spring.

Like the season which begins to blossom,
Unfolding its wide wings within our bosom
   To give us strength and divine grace,
So do you lend the world a new face
   And create around us a joyous choir
When your notes traverse the scales.

ASDRENI

With you does the shepherd climb to the mountain pastures
Moved by your magic melodies,
    Your every fire melts his heart,
With you do young lads take to the dance,
Thrilled by your sacred songs of love
    Welling anew within their breasts.

Like tender leaves quivering in the wind
Which in their rustling strike up a song
    In perfect harmony,
Whosoever hears your chant
Recalls forgotten memories
    Like a symphony from the heavens.

The farmer bent behind his plow
Or scything ripened sheaves of grain
    Knows not why he slaves,
Yet with you all his hardship dissolves
As his thirst abates when he scoops
And drinks the waters of mountain springs.

From ancient times our ancestors
Bore you in their belts, sabers brandished,
    Singing their fiery songs
And spreading courage in the thick of battle,
Always were they rewarded for their toil,
    As was the legendary Alexander.

With you did the goddess Minerva
While away the hours in delight,
    Up on flashing Olympia
And the nymphs around her like tiny stars
In the rhythmic pacing of the dance
    Teased jealous Bacchus.

Virgil, master and famed singer
Of ancient times, and Mozart—
    With you, they built their sacred altars,

With you do nations dream,
Nourished on lofty ideals
  From a healing source.

So many others have followed,
As new tokens of progress,
  Which no one on earth can oppose,
To you, poets will always weave hymns,
For with your strength and courage, magic flute,
  You soar above them all.

FAN NOLI
1882–1965

Fan Noli, also known as Theophan Stylian Noli, was not only an outstanding leader of the Albanian American community but also a preeminent and multitalented figure of Albanian literature, culture, religious life, and politics. Having emigrated to the United States, he was ordained as an Orthodox priest, and by 1912 he had become the recognized leader of the Albanian Orthodox community there, as well as an established writer and journalist of the nationalist movement. In 1919, he was selected to head an Albanian delegation to the League of Nations in Geneva, where he was successful in having Albania admitted. In 1922, he was appointed foreign minister of Albania, and on July 17, 1924, he was officially proclaimed prime minister and shortly afterward regent of Albania. For six months, he led a democratic government that tried desperately to cope with the catastrophic economic and political problems facing the young Albanian state. After his overthrow at the end of the year, he was obliged to flee abroad. He returned to the United States and withdrew from political life.

Politics and religion were not the only fields in which Fan Noli made a name for himself. He was also a dramatist, poet, historian, musicologist, and in particular an excellent translator who made a significant contribution to the development of the Albanian literary language. He has certainly not been forgotten as a poet, though his powerful declamatory verse is far from prolific. It was collected in a volume with the simple title *The Album* (*Albumi* [Boston, 1948]). The collection contains primarily political verse, well known even today, that reflects his abiding nationalist aspirations and the social and political passions of the 1920s and 1930s.

On Riverbanks

Taken flight and off in exile,
In restraints and held in bondage,
I despair with tears unending
On the banks of Spree and Elbe.

Where is it that we have left her,
Our poor homeland, wretched nation?
She lies unwashed at the seaside,
She stands unseen in the sunlight,
She sits starving at the table,
She is ignorant midst learning,
Naked, ailing does she languish,
Lame in body and in spirit . . .

How those rogues have all abused her,
How the beys and mercenaries
And the foreigners oppressed her,
How the usurers have squeezed her,
How they raged at her, destroyed her,
She from all sides has been ravaged,
Heel of force always upon her,
On the banks of Spree and Elbe.

Screaming do I burn in rage,
Bereft of weapons, mutilated,
Neither dead nor living do I
Wait here for some sign or glimmer,
Days and years I tarry, linger,
Weak and out of breath and withered,

Old before my time and broken,
Far from hearth and far from workplace,
On the banks of Rhine and Danube.

Yes, I'm beaten and bewildered,
In a swoon and in convulsions,
On I dream in tears unceasing
On the banks of Spree and Elbe.

And a voice roars from the river,
Booming, from my sleep awakes me,
That the people are now ready,
That the tyrant totters, trembles,
That a storm is rising, raging,
Vjosa swelling, Buna flooding,
Drin and Seman scarlet flowing,
Beys and nobles squirm and quiver,
For beyond the grave life shines and
Trumpets on all sides do echo:
"Rise up, set out now against them,
All you peasants and you workers,
Men from Shkodra down to Vlora,
Crush them now and overcome them!"

This salvation, yes, this war cry,
Has restored my youth and courage,
Strength and hope resuscitating,
On the banks of Spree and Elbe.
That a spring will follow winter,
That we one day will return
Regaining hearths, reclaiming workplace
On the banks of Vjosa, Buna.

Taken flight and off in exile,
In restraints and held in bondage,
I proclaim this fervent hope here
On the banks of Spree and Elbe.

FAN NOLI

Dead in Exile

Elegy written in Berlin on the death of writer and political figure
Luigj Gurakuqi (1879–1925), who had been assassinated in Bari on
March 2, 1925, by an agent of Ahmet Zogu.

O mother, mourn our brother,
Cut down by three bullets.
They mocked him, they murdered him,
They called him traitor.

For he loved you when they hated you,
For he wept when they derided you,
For he clothed you when they denuded you,
O mother, he died a martyr.

O mother, weep bitter tears,
Thugs have slain your son
Who with Ismail Qemali
Raised the valiant banner.

O mother, weep for him in Vlora,
Where he bore you freedom,
A soul as pure as snow,
For whom you have no grave.

O mother, he did his utmost
With eloquence and heart of iron,
Alive in exile, dead in exile,
This towering liberator.

Run, O Soldier of Marathon

Run, oh run, yes, speed and tell them
That the foreign hordes are beaten,
That we held out, won the battle,

With our victory saved the city,
Run, oh run,
Sprint, O soldier of Marathon!

Yes, you seized a branch of laurel,
Set off, loping down to Athens,
Over dales and through the valleys,
Hardly did your legs a-flying
Touch the ground while falling, rising,
Falcon hero, soldier of Marathon.

You are wounded, but don't feel the
Blood and sweat behind you dripping,
You're determined to be first,
To be the herald of the triumph,
Scarlet soldier of Marathon!

Your throat is dry, but you're not thirsty,
Legs are numb, but you keep vaulting,
For the people there await you,
At their hearts great fear is gnawing,
Gall and terror are within them,
Speed on, soldier of Marathon!

Never did the sun so scorch you,
Never weighed the sky so heavy,
Never were so fair and tempting
Shade of oak trees, cool springwater,
Keep on going,
Forward, soldier of Marathon!

Swirling dust and heat are stifling,
Thorns and rocks are lacerating,
In your breast burn fire and ardor,
Sweat and steam both blind your vision,
Glowing embers,
Like a torch, soldier of Marathon!

FAN NOLI

From your breast, like bellows heaving,
Smoke and sparks of a volcano
Belching forth and wide resounding,
Like a maul your heart is pounding
'gainst your ribs, be
Steadfast, soldier of Marathon!

Mothers, sisters, and young women
Swarm and raise their arms to stop you,
Do not listen, they're but naiads,
Witches doing magic, dryads,
Keep your distance,
Fly on, soldier of Marathon!

Now before you the Acropolis,
Both the city and people
Have now spotted, recognized you,
Giving you new strength and courage,
Keep on going,
Rush on, soldier of Marathon!

You arrive, proudly proclaim the
Cruel joy of that great message,
Crying: "We won!" having spoken,
Fall to earth in last convulsions,
Dead and perished!
Perished, soldier of Marathon!

Run forever blithe announcing
To the glory of the ages
That a lad has felled a giant,
Those oppressed have slain a tyrant,
All alone and all in union,
Union, soldier of Marathon!

LASGUSH PORADECI
1899–1987

Lasgush Poradeci is the unforgotten bard of Lake Ohrid. He was raised in the town of Pogradec, not far from where, at the foot of the "Mal i Thatë" (Dry Mountain), the Drin River takes its source and but a few kilometers from the famed medieval monastery of Saint Naum's, now just over the Macedonian border. The lake never ceased to fascinate and enchant him. He studied its hues, the reflection of light both upon its waves and in the depths of its sparkling waters, and observed how the surrounding mountains cast their shadows over it.

Poradeci is the author of two extraordinary collections of poetry. *The Dance of the Stars* (*Vallja e yjve*) and *The Star of the Heart* (*Ylli i zemrës*), published in Romania in 1933 and 1937, respectively, contain some of the most melodious and metrically refined poetry ever written in Albanian. Poradeci's subjects, together with his structures and language, were very much attuned to southern Albanian oral literature, in particular to Tosk folk verse, from which he drew a good deal of his inspiration.

Pogradec

A shimmering sunset on the endless lake.
Ghostlike, a veil is slowly spread.
Over mountain and meadow the dark of night descends,
Settling from the heavens upon the town.

Over the vast land no more sound is to be heard:
In the village the creaking of a door,
On the lake the silence of an oar.
Over the Mal i Thatë an elusive eagle soars.
My youthful heart retreats into the depths of my soul.

The whole town, all life, retires to the realm of sleep.
Darkness rules the four quarters of the earth. And now,
Setting out on his journey through Albania,
Legendary Father Drin arises at Saint Naum's.

Morning

Like a spirit somber within the breast
Lies the lake encased in hills.
Mirrored in its depths,
Night expires breath by breath.

I watch how she suffers, how she dies,
Her eyes blinking,
Azure-circled pools,
Like the stars of a fading sky.

But now the light of dawn
Shimmers deep within the lake.
The daystar steals away, melting
Like a piece of sugar candy.

Behold, day has dawned,
And lightning flashes from the depths.
Like a harbinger of morn
Appears, bird-white, a pelican.

End of Autumn

The last stork flew off, majestic and forlorn,
Soaring over the snowy mountains at the break of day,
After tapping on the door with his sturdy beak,
Leaving his nest to the master's care and departing heavy of heart.

No longer does the fateful bird comb the plowed fields,
The furrows cut into the soil by mountain oxen,
No longer is the gray mouse heard scurrying over fallow land,
In the barren brake the speckled snake is dead.

Beneath the icy wind, the hoary earth lies silent,
The north wind howls through the withered trees.
As the cold grips harder, a clever little wren
Chatters blithely over hedge and over sedge.

Oh, how graceful was the stork, how slender and noble,
Pacing slowly like a bridegroom crowned!
At his side, with radiant breast, the crane,
With measured step, eyes uplifted—played his bride!

Winter

From today my spirit is a recluse,
And banished is all my joy.
Long has it been that snow has lain
Over mountain and over wood.

Snowflakes come drifting one by one
Down upon the deserted village
And, shivering beneath the snow,
Earth slumbers, buried once again.

Slowly my spirit too sinks to the ground
In mourning, falling like a leaf.
Nary a soul is to be heard,
No people, no sign of life.

In such peace and tranquillity
I hear a bird lament,
Letting out a faint sigh,
Frightened to leave this life.

LASGUSH PORADECI

SEJFULLAH MALËSHOVA
1901–1971

Originally from the Përmet region of southern Albania, Sejfullah Malëshova, who used the pen name Lame Kodra, spent a good deal of his life abroad. He studied medicine in Italy and in 1924, at the age of twenty-three, became Fan Noli's personal secretary in the latter's democratic government. A left-wing revolutionary, Malëshova was conferred with the initial responsibility for cultural policies after the Communist takeover of Albania in 1944. He followed a relatively liberal and conciliatory course in order to encourage the reintegration of non-Communist forces into the new structures of power, but to no avail. Purged in 1946, this idealist who had once been a member of the Comintern was interned in Ballsh for two or three years and spent all his later life in internal exile as a humble stock clerk in Fier, where, for years, no inhabitant of the town dared speak to him. His only social contact was playing soccer with the children. Whenever anyone approached, he would pinch his lips with his fingers, signifying the vow of eternal silence that ensured his survival. Sejfullah Malëshova died in 1971 of appendicitis in unimaginable isolation. Although everyone in town knew his poems by heart, no one dared to attend his funeral. He was buried in the presence of the gravedigger, two Sigurimi agents, and his sister.

Most of the verse of this self-styled rebel poet was written in exile and published in the volume *Verse (Vjersha* [Tirana, 1945]).

How I Love Albania

I've no farm estates or manors,
I've no shops or lofty buildings,
Yet I love my land, Albania—
For a barn in Trebeshina,
For its boulders and its brushwood,
For a hut above Selishta,
For two fields plowed in Zallishta,

For a cow and for a donkey,
For an ox, a little lambkin,
   This is how I love my country
   Like a shepherd, like a peasant.

Yes, I love my land, Albania,
For the clover in its meadows,
For a quick and agile maiden,
For its spring of water gurgling
From the cliffs and flowing swiftly
Through the leafy oak tree forests,
Tumbling down to form a river,
Yes, I love my land, Albania,
For the fenugreek in blossom,
For the birds that fly above it,
For the nightingales a-singing,
In the shade and in the brambles,
Trilling songs of love and longing,
   This is how I love my country,
   Like a poet in devotion.

Yes, I love my land, Albania,
Right from Korça to Vranina,
Where the farmer sets off early
With his hoe and plow a-toiling,
Sows and reaps by sun and moonlight,
Yet, he has no food to live on,
Where the farrier and saddler
Day and night stoop o'er their duties
Just to get a few stale breadcrumbs,
Where the porter at the dockyards,
Laden down with iron and barrels,
Bears his load, barefoot and ragged,
Always serving other people.
Yes, I love my land, Albania,
Right from Skopje to Janina,
Where its people in misfortune

SEJFULLAH MALËSHOVA

Suffer, live their lives in serfdom,
Yet they have a fighting spirit—
    This is how I love my country,
    Like a revolutionary.

Rebel Poet

Listen to me, men and women,
    Everywhere,
There's a warrant out to snare me
    from Tirana.
Over hill and over dale and
    in the fields,
Their patrols are right behind me
    step by step.
I fear not their hunting dogs and
    all their guns,
I am off and make my journey
    path by path,
I am off and will find shelter
    house by house,
Everywhere in this, my country,
    I've my lair.
I'm a thug and I'm a rebel
    and I'm proud,
Both the beys and, yes, their thrones I
    will attack.
I have come to do my job,
    protect the poor,
And a war on slavery have I
    now declared.

■ □ ■

Who have raised their guns against me?
    let me know!

Who's behind me, searching for my
    every trace?
Stop a while and listen to me,
    soldier boy,
Are you not a peasant's son, a
    village lad?
Bide a bit and listen to me,
    brother mine,
Hold your pace and save your bullet
    for those men,
For the ones who rob, oppress our
    piteous home,
For the ones who here exhaust us
    in our plight.
And my poems may, too, resemble
    me, a thug,
For my lines with black gunpowder
    have I filled.
Songs of war and songs of fire
    in my mouth,
And a storehouse full of weapons
    is my chest,
Verse, my verse, fly off in fury
    like a bomb,
Go and furl out like a war cry,
    like a flag,
Let our country's people gather
    everywhere,
Let the tyrant tremble, quiver
    in his hall.
To your feet arise, O Korça,
    matriarch,
With Devoll and with Kolonja,
    with Opar.
Come forth now, O Vlora River,
    banner high,
As you'd come to pick your bride up
    in her veil,

SEJFULLAH MALËSHOVA

To the vanguard like Gjoleka,
    Kurvelesh,
Beat upon them, Chameria,
    like a storm.
Like an earthquake may you bellow,
    Mount Tomorr,
May the waves of Shkumbin River
    seethe and boil.
Rise up, people, like a lion,
    Cast the yoke,
In Berat and in Tirana,
    Elbasan,
And you, Mat, Luma, and Dibra,
    like the wind,
Seize your arms and for your freedom
    take to war,
Moan and groan, O wretched Shkodra,
    ancient town,
Come along, arise Kosova,
    join the dance,
With Krasniqi, Bajram Curri
    and Tetova.
Let our country's people gather
    everywhere,
Let the tyrant tremble, quiver
    in his hall.
Verse, my verse, fly off in fury
    like a bomb,
Go and furl out like a war cry,
    like a flag.

MITRUSH KUTELI
1907–1967

Mitrush Kuteli, pseudonym of Dhimitër Pasko, was born in Pog-
radec, on the banks of Lake Ohrid, and emigrated to Romania.

He began publishing the collections of short stories for which he is best known in Bucharest. In the autumn of 1942, he returned to Albania and published a verse collection, *Assault and Tears* (*Sulm e lotë* [Tirana, 1944]). An executive at the Albanian State Bank, Kuteli was also a leading figure of Albanian letters at the time of the Communist takeover. He managed to survive the transition of power in the country until the real terror began in 1947. During the purge, which ensued when the Albanian Communists came under Yugoslav domination, he was arrested and sentenced to fifteen years in prison. He spent two years of his sentence in a labor camp near Korça, where inmates were put to work draining the infamous mosquito-infested swamp of Maliq. With the elimination of Yugoslav influence in Albanian party politics, however, the open persecution of Kuteli subsided and he was released. He returned to Tirana and was allowed to work as a literary translator for the state-owned Naim Frashëri publishing company. He died of a heart attack in Tirana, bereft of the honor and recognition due to the man who, had politics not interfered, might otherwise have been a major literary figure of the fifties.

The Muddy Albanian Soil

I love you, muddy Albanian soil,
I love you
Ferociously,
Desperately,
Like a wolf loves the forest,
Like a wave loves a wave,
Like mud loves mud.

Up to my knees
I am into you,
For I was born
Here,
Like my father,
Like my grandfather,

I love you, muddy Albanian soil,
Up to my waist
And above it,
I am into you,
And I cannot stop
For I do not wish to.

For you bind me
And captivate me
With honey
And with wormwood.

For my mother
And my father
And my ancestors
All perished
Here.

I love you, muddy Albanian soil,
Magic,
And sweet,
Like death itself.

For I am deep here,
Deep into you,
Up to my knees,
Up to my waist,
And up to my neck.

And how I would love to get drunk
And relax
(Right now!)
Within you.

To hug you
Desperate,
To embrace you,
To be embraced,

Ferociously,
Desperately
That you absorb me
As you absorbed
My ancestors, absorbed
O my noble-minded,
Gray-haired,
Withered-bodied
Father.

I love you, muddy Albanian soil,
Magic,
Sweet as honey,
Bitter as wormwood,
I love you
Ferociously,
Desperately,
Like a wolf loves the forest,
Like a wave loves a wave,
Like mud loves mud!

MIGJENI
1911–1938

With Migjeni, pen name of Millosh Gjergj Nikolla, contemporary Albanian poetry begins its course. Migjeni was born in Shkodra and attended a Serbian Orthodox elementary school. In the autumn of 1925, he obtained a scholarship to attend a secondary school in Monastir (Bitola) in southern Macedonia. Upon graduating in 1927, he entered the Orthodox Seminary of St. John the Theologian, also in Monastir, where, despite incipient health problems, he continued his training and studies until June 1932. Following his return to Shkodra in 1932, he failed to win a scholarship to study in the "wonderful West" and decided to take up a teaching career rather than join the priesthood for which he had been trained. It was during this period that he also began writing verse and prose sketches that reflect the life and anguish of an intellectual in what certainly was the most backward region of Europe. Sick with tuberculosis, the poet was soon obliged to put an end to his career as a teacher and as a writer and to seek medical treatment in northern Italy. After five months at San Luigi sanatorium near Turin, Migjeni was transferred to a hospital in Torre Pellice, where he died at the age of twenty-six.

It is as a poet that Migjeni made his mark on Albanian literature and culture, though he did so posthumously. The main theme of his only volume of verse, *Free Verse* (*Vargjet e lira* [Tirana, 1944]), composed over a three-year period from 1933 to 1935, is misery and suffering. It is a poetry of acute social awareness and despair. Previous generations of poets had sung the beauties of the Albanian mountains and the sacred traditions of the nation, whereas Migjeni opened his eyes to the harsh realities of life, to the appalling level of misery, disease, and poverty he discovered all around him. He was a poet of despair who saw no way out, who cherished no hope that anything but death could put an end to suffering.

Poem of Poverty

Poverty, brothers, is a mouthful that's hard to swallow,
A bite that sticks in your throat and leaves you in sorrow,
When you watch the pale faces and rheumy eyes
Observing you like ghosts and holding out thin hands;
Behind you they lie, stretched out
Their whole lives through, until the moment of death.
Above them in the air, as if in disdain,
Crosses and stony minarets pierce the sky,
Prophets and saints in many colors radiate splendor.
And poverty feels betrayed.

Poverty carries its own vile imprint,
It is hideous, repulsive, disgusting.
The brow that bears it, the eyes that express it,
The lips that try in vain to hide it

Are the offspring of ignorance, the victims of disdain,
The filthy scraps flung from the table
At which for centuries
Some pitiless, insatiable dog has fed.
Poverty has no good fortune, only rags,
The tattered banners of a hope
Shattered by broken promises.

Poverty wallows in debauchery.
In dark corners, together with dogs, rats, cats,
On moldy, stinking, filthy mattresses,
Naked breasts exposed, sallow, dirty bodies,
With feelings overwhelmed by bestial desire,
They bite, devour, suck, kiss the sullied lips,
And in unbridled lust the thirst is quenched,
The craving stilled, and self-consciousness lost.
Here is the source of the imbeciles, the servants, and the beggars
Who will tomorrow be born to fill the streets.

Poverty shines in the eyes of the newborn,
Flickers like the pale flame of a candle
Under a ceiling blackened with smoke and spider webs,
Where human shadows tremble on damp stained walls,
Where the ailing infant wails like a banshee
To suck the dry breasts of its wretched mother
Who, pregnant again, curses god and the devil,
Curses the heavy burden of her unborn child.
Her baby does not laugh, it only wastes away,
Unwanted by its mother, who curses it, too.
How sorrowful is the cradle of the poor
Where a child is rocked with tears and sighs.

Poverty's child is raised in the shadows
Of great mansions, too high for imploring voices to reach
To disturb the peace and quiet of the lords
Sleeping in blissful beds beside their ladies.

Poverty matures a child before its time,
Teaches it to dodge the threatening fist,
The hand which clutches its throat in dreams,
When the delirium of starvation begins
And when death casts its shadow on childish faces,
Instead of a smile a hideous grimace.
While the fate of a fruit is to ripen and fall,
The child is interred not maturing at all.

Poverty labors and toils by day and night,
Chest and forehead drenched in sweat,
Up to the knees in mud and slime,
And still the empty guts writhe in hunger.
Starvation wages! For such a daily ordeal,
A mere three or four leks and an "On your way."

Poverty sometimes paints its face,
Swollen lips scarlet, hollow cheeks rouged,
And body a chattel in a filthy trade.
For service in bed for which it is paid
With a few lousy francs,
Stained sheets, stained face, and stained conscience.

Poverty leaves a heritage as well,
Not cash in the bank or property you can sell,
But distorted bones and pains in the chest,
Perhaps leaves the memory of a bygone day
When the roof of the house, weakened by decay,
By age and the weather collapsed and fell,
And above all the din rose a terrible cry
Cursing and imploring, as from the depths of hell,
The voice of a man crushed by a beam.
Under the heel, says the priest, of a god irate
Ends thus the life of a dissolute ingrate.
And so the memory of such misfortunes
Fills the cup of bitterness passed to generations.

Poverty in drink seeks consolation,
In filthy taverns, with dirty, littered tables,
The thirsting soul pours glass after glass
Down the throat to forget its many worries,
The dulling glass, the glass satanic,
Caressing with a venomous bite.
And when, like grain under the scythe, the man falls
To the floor, he giggles and sobs, a tragicomic clown,
And all his sorrow in drink he drowns
When one by one, a hundred glasses downs.

Poverty sets desires ablaze like stars in the night
And turns them to ashes, like trees struck by lightning.

Poverty knows no joy, but only pain,
Pain reducing you to such despair
That you seize the rope and hang yourself,
Or become a poor victim of "paragraphs."

Poverty wants no pity, only justice!
Pity? Bastard daughter of cunning fathers,
Who like the Pharisees, beating the drum
Ostentatiously for their own sly ends,
Drop a penny in the beggar's hands.

Poverty is an indelible stain
On the brow of humanity through the ages.
And never can this stain be effaced
By doctrines decaying in temples.

Blasphemy

The mosques and churches float through our memories,
Prayers devoid of sense or taste echo from their walls.
Never has the heart of god been touched by them,
And yet it beats on amidst the sounds of drums and bells.

Majestic mosques and churches throughout our wretched land,
Spires and minarets towering over lowly homes,
The voice of the hodjas and priest in one degenerate chant,
O ideal vision, a thousand years old!

The mosques and churches float through memories of the pious,
The chiming of the bell mingles with the muezzin's call,
Sanctity shines from cowls and from the beards of hodjas.
O so many fair angels at the gates of hell!

On ancient citadels perch carrion ravens,
Their dejected wings drooping—the symbols of lost hopes,
In despair do they croak of an age gone by
When the ancient citadels once gleamed with hallowed joy.

Song of Noble Grief

O noble grief of the suffering soul
That into free verse bursts out . . .
Would you perchance take comfort
In adorning the world with jewels?

O noble grief in free verse,
Which sincerely sounds and resounds,
Will you ever move the feelings of men,
Or wither and die like the autumn leaves?

O song worthy of noble grief . . .
Never rest! But with your twin,
Lamentation, sing out your suffering,
For time will be your consolation.

Autumn on Parade

Autumn in nature and autumn in our faces.
The sultry breeze enfeebles, the glowering sun
Oppresses the ailing spirit in our breasts,
Shrivels the life trembling among the twigs of a poplar.

The yellow colors twirl in the final dance,
(A frantic desire of leaves dying one by one).
Our joys, passions, our ultimate desires
Fall and are trampled in the autumn mud.

An oak tree, reflected in the tears of heaven,
Tosses and bleeds in gigantic passion.
"To live! I want to live!"—it fights for breath,
Piercing the storm with cries of grief.

The horizon, drowned in fog, joins in
The lamentation. In prayer dejected fruit trees
Fold imploring branches—but in vain, they know.
Tomorrow they will die . . . Is there nowhere hope?

The eye is saddened. Saddened, too, the heart
At the hour of death, when silent fall the veins
And from the grave to the highest heavens soar
Despairing cries of long-unheeded pain.

Autumn in nature and autumn in our faces.
Moan, desires, offspring of poverty,
Groan in lamentation, bewail the corpses,
That adorn this autumn among the withered branches.

Scandalous Song

A pale-faced nun who with the sins of this world
Bears my sins, too, upon her weary shoulders,
Those shoulders, wan as wax, which some deity has kissed,
Roams the streets like a fleeting angel.

A pale-faced nun, cold as a marble tomb,
With grayish eyes like the ashes of spent desires,
With thin red-ribbon lips, tightly pressed to smother her sighs,
A chilling image of her has lingered in my memory.

From pious prayers she comes and to her prayers she returns.
In downcast eyes, in lips, in folded hands her prayers repose.
Without her prayers what fate would be the world's?
Yet they cannot stop another day from dawning.

O nun so pale, making love to the saints,
Consumed in ecstasy before them like an altar candle,
Revealing herself to them . . . , oh, how I envy the saints,
Pray not for me, for I am hell-bent with desire.

You and I, nun, are two ends of a rope,
On which two teams tug one against the other—
The struggle is stern and who knows how it will end,
So, tug the rope, let the teams contend.

Resignation

In tears have we found consolation. . . .
Our heritage in life has been
Misery . . . for this whole world
Is but a grave in the universal womb,
Where human reptiles are condemned to creep,
Their will crushed in the grip of a giant.
—An eye adorned in purest tears of profound pain

Shines from the far side of hell,
And at times, the reflection of a fleeting thought
Flashes round the globe
To give vent to awesome wrath.
But the head hangs, the sorrowful eyelids droop
And through the lashes wells a crystal tear,
Rolls down the cheek and splashes on the earth,
And in every splash of a teardrop a man is born
To take to the road of his own destiny.
In the hope of the smallest victory, he roams from land to land,
Over roads covered with brambles, among which he passes
Graves washed in tears and crazy folk who snigger.

Fragment

. . . .
. . . .
. . . .
On the mercy of the merciless
The little beggar survived.
His life ran its course
In dirty streets,
In dark corners,
In cold doorways,
Among fallacious faiths.
But one day, when the world's pity dried up,
He felt in his breast the stab
Of a new pain, which contempt
Fosters in the hearts
Of the poor.
And, though yesterday a little beggar,
He now became something new.
An avenger of the past,
He conceived an imprecation
To pronounce to the world,
His throat strained

MIGJENI

To bring out the word
Which his rage had gripped
And smothered on his lips.
Speechless he sat
At the crossroads,
When the wheels of a passing car
Quickly crushed
And . . . silenced him.

The Themes

Is there the theme of a poem among fading memories,
Among the happy memories of childhood innocence,
When the heart was full of worldly pleasures,
Desires, hopes, and ever-sweet dreams?

Is there the fiery theme of a poem of love
Among the lingering memories of eager youth,
With sonorous rhymes and ardent vows,
Full of the lust for life and shouts of mirth?

On the pallid faces of fallen women
Loitering in doorways to sell themselves,
On their faces a tragic poem is carved
In tears and grief that rise to the heavens,

In dark corners where derision reigns
In disgust, and the insane jeer
At their wives and children,
There in revolt great themes await creation.

In hidden corners where fear dwells
And passivity lurks to smother life,
There in betrayal does the theme take its source
And with it, the poet pens his verse.

Throughout man's life do themes of all kinds
Come and go. Now the ultimate of themes has come,
Frightening in our fantasy—the paling of the face,
An ominous shadow, and the death knell tolls.

Suffering

For some time now
I have seen clearly
How from suffering my eyes are growing larger,
The furrows in my face and brow are growing deeper,
And my smile has grown bitter . . .
. . . and I have come to realize
That the coming days
Will no longer be constructive ones
Of energy and work, but simply the passing
Of a waning life.

With time, I have come to see
How this treacherous life
Has singed
Each of my senses,
One by one,
Until nothing remains
Of the joy
I once had.

O life,
I did not know before
How much I dreaded
Your grip
That strangles
Ruthless.

But helpless now,
I gaze into the mirror and see
How from suffering my eyes are growing larger,
The furrows in my face and brow are growing deeper,
And that soon I will become
A tattered banner,
Worn and torn
In the battles of life.

Under the Banners of Melancholy

The banners
Of a mournful melancholy
Wave
Throughout our land . . .
Nor can it be said
That here live a people
Who are building
Something new.
Here and there in the shadow
Of the banners
An effort can be seen,
A gigantic struggle
To triumph over death,
To give birth to something great,
To bring a jinni to light!
But (O irony of fate)
From all that labor
Only a mouse is born.
And thus this comedy
Bursts our vein of humor,
And we ourselves
Burst into rage.
Over the threshold of each house
That contains a sign of life

Mournful melancholy
Unfolds its banner.

ESAD MEKULI
1916–1993

The writer widely considered to be the father of modern Albanian poetry in what was Yugoslavia, Esad Mekuli was born in the mountain village of Plava, on the Montenegrin-Albanian border. He went to school in Peja, on the Kosovar side of the wild Rugova canyon, and studied veterinary medicine at the University of Belgrade. There he came into contact with Marxist teachings and subsequently took part in the partisan movement of World War II. In 1949, he founded the literary periodical *New Life* (*Jeta e Re*), whose editor in chief he remained until 1971. Mekuli was a committed poet of social awareness whose outrage at injustice, violence, genocide, and suffering mirrored that of the prerevolutionary verse of the messianic Migjeni of Shkodra. His first collection, *For You* (*Për ty* [Prishtina, 1955]), was dedicated to the people of Kosova. His final collection, *The Light That Does Not Go Out* (*Drita që nuk shuhet* [Prishtina, 1989]), appeared over thirty years later. Mekuli also published translations of much Yugoslav literature, including the works of the Montenegrin poet-prince Petar Njegoš (1813–51) as well as Serbian translations of many volumes of Albanian literature.

Is It the Albanian's Fault?

On hearing of the secret agreement to expel four hundred thousand so-called Turks from "southern Serbia" to the wilds of Anatolia, sixty-five Kosovar students (fifty-six Serbs and Montenegrins, eight Albanians, and one Turk) signed and published a protest (in Serbo-Croatian and Albanian) against the Yugoslav government for this crime against the people. The protest was transmitted illicitly to foreign embassies in Belgrade and distributed throughout Kosova and Macedonia.

Is it the Albanian's fault that he lives under this sky,
Under this sky, in the land of his ancestors?
Is it his fault that he exists and will not be uprooted,
The Albanian, slave or master, who wants to belong to himself?

Is it the Albanian's fault that his eyes flash fire
When he glares as others expel him from his home and his soil?
Is it his fault that he exists when others wish him dead,
Or that he will spill blood to defend his hearth and not give up
      alive?

Is it the Albanian's fault that he wishes to live as others do,
Like a human being, among his own people, now and forever?
Is it his fault that, despite force, he resists
Under the precious sky of Kosova, the land of his ancestors?

Evening

Like the golden fringes of an azure shawl
Held in two white hands, two snow-laden hills,
The sunset flames . . . Overhead the clouds
Cross the sky and melt into space.

As the last rays fade over the slopes,
The veil spreads to cover the ash-gray plains,
The mountains now fall silent, frozen and
Lifeless . . . All things have grown somber and vanish.

Night has fallen and, in the air, cries can be heard,
The trees by the roadside tremble in the wind. . . .
Yet in some distant land is the white light of dawn

Whetting its golden arrows to overwhelm the night.
Darkness reigns o'er the world. In the valley, the villages,
Stretched out in the wee hours, are sound asleep.

The Death of Day

The setting sun
Spent itself
In a flickering fire. . . .

All things quivered
In sadness
And lamentation.

In that silent coffin of twilight,
In orphaned pain
Tonight

We mourned
What we loved, what was ours,
With pristine tears.

The sighing of the blades of grass,
The quiet sobbing of the wind
Met my heart in sorrow. . . .
The sun tonight
Spent itself
In a flickering fire.

I

I know no joy: worry seethes in my heart,
I am alone—no brother or sister,
A broken child on the misty horizon
Where lightning flashes and flings one into the depths.

I am the pain of the poor, bereft of food and drink,
A mother's tear fallen on an empty table,
I am the longing of the slave, forever pursued,
Who rises like a giant in the air amongst the birch trees.

ESAD MEKULI

I am the suffering of the oppressed, muffled in misery,
A war cry resounding, scattering all impediments,
In that great expectation splendidly arising
Over the ruins, I am a ray of hope.

No, I know no joy, worry seethes in my heart,
I am alone—no brother or sister,
A broken child on the misty horizon
Where lightning flashes and flings one into the depths.

Hope

> Two fishermen, covered in a piece of torn canvas and rocked by the
> waves, are asleep in their tiny boat called *Ümüt* (*Hope*), the letters
> of which can hardly be read.

All night long did the foaming waves beat them,
The beacon its signal did cast,
Yet they, caught in reverie visions,
Had drifted and fallen asleep,

Outstretched,
A brief respite
In their struggle for a better life,
For that which they longed to lead.

. . . Then the dawn cast its white rays,
The sun outshone the lighthouse,
Wide-eyed gulls perched on the reefs.

Alone were the two of them, waiting
In their Hope, rocked in their reverie,
And in their endless dreams.

ARSHI PIPA
1920–1997

Writer and scholar Arshi Pipa was born in Shkodra. His first poetry, composed in the late 1930s in Shkodra, was collected in the volume *Sailors* (*Lundërtarë* [Tirana, 1944]). Pipa studied philosophy at the University of Florence, receiving his doctor of philosophy degree in 1942 with a dissertation on Henri Bergson (1859–1941). Following his studies, he worked as a teacher in Shkodra and Tirana. Unwilling to conform after the radical transition of power at the end of World War II, he was arrested in April 1946 and imprisoned for ten years. After his release in 1956, he escaped to Yugoslavia and emigrated to the United States two years later. He held teaching posts at various U.S. universities and, until his retirement, was professor of Italian at the University of Minnesota in Minneapolis. Pipa digested his ten years of horror in the prisons and labor camps of Durrës, Vloçisht, Gjirokastra, and Burrel in *The Prison Book* (*Libri i burgut* [Rome, 1959]), a 246-page collection of verse. He has published two other volumes of poetry in the Gheg dialect: *Rusha* (Munich, 1968) and *Meridiana* (Munich, 1969), the latter a collection in the romantic and nostalgic vein of Giacomo Leopardi.

The First Night

A kitchen, not in use for ages,
Over the sink with its porcelain tiles,
An oil lamp coughs black smoke,
The door locked, the windows sealed.

A cluster of shadows low along the wall,
A chamber pot behind the door, near it some old
Onion skins, a rat gnawing on crumbs of bread,
Someone gulping from a flask.

The shadows shift, curious eyes and faces
Emerge from cloaks and shawls,
A heavy step shakes the stairs. Silence.

A clank of dead bolts, a scream near the office,
Another howl, frightening and long, followed
By demeaning curses. Then the bolts again . . . and steps . . .

Dawn

The dawns cannot be seen,
Can only be heard.
Slumber, anguish, waking
In horror . . . a jumble

Of snoring guards, sweat,
And fumes of gas,
With cries, with clamor,
And the stench of decay.

And now from the other side,
A beckoning voice,
A long whisper.

Whistling, chirping,
The birds in the pines
Bid good-bye to the night.

The Lamp

I entreat you, do not close the window,
O unknown woman,
I dream of your movements,
Of your voice evoking spring!

I beg you, do not snuff out the lamp,
I crave it tonight,
My hope in the gloom,
Like a sail untouched by the wind.

The Canal

Thunder near Korça. The rain courses
Down tarpaulins onto heads, upon the hay,
The prisoners huddle, cower in their covers,
A heap of putrid flesh and rags.

Evening has come. Blood streams from a mouth,
A gypsy lad sings oblivious his song,
Some scuffle over a scoop of water slurped by a comrade,
Others curse for a bite of stolen bread. A guard enters,

Kicking and thrashing, cries, a whistle blows.
Then calm. All are exhausted,
Try to catch some sleep if they can.

Groans and sighs from the first-aid barracks.
In the morn, the canal and the marsh will be biding,
Except for those awaited by a barren grave.

■ □ ■ □ ■

CONTEMPORARY VERSE

ZEF ZORBA
1920–1993

The literary significance of the poetic works of Zef Zorba was discovered only after his death. He has since joined the ranks of the great writers of classic Albanian poetry stifled by the Communist regime.

Zef Zorba was born in Kotor, in Montenegro, of an Albanian family. He finished secondary school in Shkodra and, in 1941, began his studies in political science at the University of Padua. The events of World War II forced him to abandon his university education and to return to Shkodra in 1943, where he worked initially for a bank. From 1945 to 1946, he served as director of the House of Culture in Shkodra, where he was responsible for the staging of plays, works that soon came to be regarded as a threat to the new Communist authorities. It is perhaps for this reason that he was arrested in 1946 and charged with agitation and propaganda. Zorba spent the following years in labor and "reeducation" camps, until his release in 1951. Thereafter he kept a low profile and worked modestly as a bookkeeper for the Shkodra district administration until his retirement in 1980. Zorba is the author of poetry, plays, libretti, and essays. Of his literary works, only one volume has been published, the slim but much appreciated collection *Lips Frozen in Joy* (*Buzë të ngrira në gaz* [Tirana, 1994]).

Somber This Path

Somber this path. I cannot
Find my way without your
Light (What is this twinge?).

At the edge of the chasm
What lure and temptation,
Can't you see how I teeter?

A Moment, Poetry: Life

Light in the mist.

I discern your face, powdery snow,
Bashful and a slight smile
Like protoplasm "in vitro,"

But it is swallowed by this swirl of dryads,
Leaving naught but an inkling.

Yearning

On such nights
At Qafë-Hardhi
The shrubs
Are freckled
With the fancies
Of fireflies.

Feast Tonight

Feast tonight: rain and storm,
Thunder and winds from Lezha,
(no moon).

On the cement before me
The raindrops beat in fury,
The hail shatters like salt,
O cement, I'm so like you.

Like Swallows

The dusk now is hastily
Drenching my road,
(those lines of light have gone crazy somewhere).

Sorrow from my brain
Foams and floods
Into my weary limbs.

I pull at my leg, it drags behind.

Like swallows
The children of the neighborhood
Wing along beside me,
Soaked in strength and joy.

The Gravel of the Kir

White gravel, bereft of light,
Where at nighttime, thousands
Of stars descend
Unheard.

Perhaps they are eyes,
The stares of children
Who died of wonder.

Kruja

Seen from Fushë-Kruja by night

A garland of daisies
On your sallow
Breast,

O my country.

Roads in Autumn

Complex canyons
In which the wind raves,
Amassing on doorsteps
Billows of dead leaves,
Mad tales.

A Nail

A nail thrust knifelike into the wall, a nail
Thrust knifelike into the wall, a nail thrust,

A nail driven deep inside the wall, a nail
Driven deep inside the wall, a nail driven,

A nail left rusting in the wall, a nail
Left rusting in the wall, a nail left,

Thrust knifelike . . .
Driven deep . . .
Left rusting . . .

MARTIN CAMAJ
1925–1992

Martin Camaj was born in Temali, in the Dukagjin region of the northern Albanian alps. He is an émigré writer of significance for both Albanian literature and Albanian scholarship. Camaj received a classical education at the Jesuit Xaverian college in Shkodra and studied at the University of Belgrade. He undertook postgraduate research in Italy, where he taught Albanian and finished, in 1960, his studies in linguistics at the University of Rome. From 1970 to 1990, he was professor of Albanian studies at the University of Munich and lived in the mountain village of Lenggries, in upper Bavaria, until his death.

Camaj's first volumes of classical verse, published in Prishtina, were inspired by his native northern Albanian mountains, for which he never lost his attachment despite long years of exile and the impossibility of return. These were followed by *Legends* (*Legjenda* [Rome, 1964]) and *Lyrics Between Two Ages* (*Lirika mes dy moteve* [Munich, 1967]). His mature verse reflects the influence of the Hermetic movement of Italian poet Giuseppe Ungaretti (1888–1970). The metaphoric and symbolic character of Camaj's language increased with time, as did the range of his poetic themes. A selection of his poetry has been translated into English by Leonard Fox (*Selected Poetry* [New York: New York University Press, 1990] and *Palimpsest* [New York: n.p., 1991]).

Mountain Feast

Blood was avenged today.
Two bullets felled a man.

Blood was avenged today.

Under the axe head
The ox's skull bursts by the stream.
(Today there will be great feasting!)

Blood was avenged today.

The wailing of men gone wild
Mingles with the smell of meat on the fires.
And the autumn foliage falls
Scorched on the white caps
At the tables, outside.

Night. At the graves on the hill
Fresh earth, new moon.

The wolves have descended from the mountains
And drink blood at the stream.

First Elegy

When I am exhausted
By the tribulations of age, steep like a cliff,
Feel no pain for me, Taze,
Stretched out on the bier,
A lamb ready for sacrifice.
Let the old women mourn over me that day
For their own people long since dead.

And one more request, my wife:
When my father died, we slaughtered two oxen
To feed the starving—and the ants of the threshing floor
With bread crumbs.
But I shall die amidst people who are
Always full,
So at my wake serve
Only bitter coffee.

A Bird Languishes

The Canon of Birds says:
Every bird shall stretch its wings and perish on the grass,
Punishment for having plied the forbidden border
Between heaven and earth.

A bird languishes upon the lawn, at death's door,
The leaves in the trees are
Unreachable birds and companions
Frolicking in the sunlight.

In the distance are two millstones pounding
At one another, as is their wont,
Silently.

Disregard

After midnight the moon casts its beams
From the cliff top to the river below.
Half asleep
The little owl sings in the rays:
Eyes, two drops of water, sparkle, and the song
Drips into the valley, the darkness.

At dawn, someone on the riverbank found
The broken beak of the little owl and stammered:
"Oh! Look at that vowel that fell
And shattered on the rocks."

Death—Crackling

Death—the crackling
Of a dry leaf,
Wait for me at the end of the earth
With no chrysanthemum in your hand.

Wait, benumbed swallow,
With wings o'er the waves, for my breath

To soar to the heavens,
Feathered like a white raven.

Unexpected Guest in Berisha

When the guest entered the house at dusk,
Seven brothers looked askance
As if he were walking over their heads and not
Over the dry floorboards. Nor did they, as ancient custom demands,
Greet and speak with him, but stared at the ground.

The youngest of them broke the silence,
Removed the *lahuta* from its place
And laid it in the guest's lap for him to play.
When he held the lute's body,
Gently stroking its side
With his rough fingers,
And plucked its foal-hair string with his thumb,
The brothers and the old man, head of the household,
Understood that the stranger was a singer
Like no other among them.

The beginning holds the heart in sway,
Not the end of the song.

Avalanche

At six o'clock in the morning
It still withstood the storm.
At noon the forest, the face
Of the mountain, plunged into the river.

The sun came out and shone on the fresh earth,
The ruptured roots, the shattered trees
And the end of my conscience.

The inhabitants of the mountains on the other side asked:
"Frail land, where can we now hide our eyes
On your treeless brow?"

Winter

Snowflakes in the treetops
And spring heather swathed in ice,
The eye searches for a hidden fire,
The badger its lair
In the womb of roots and remembers
The warmth of breath
Under a white sheep's hide.

The hedgehog with its spines embedded deep in flesh
Flickers without a flame
Within the four walls of the earth.

My Mother

The dry sumac quivers
On the promontory above the Drin, drubbed
By the savage winds of Saint Andrew's Day.
And she declares to me: "You're a dead weight
In my breast!

Cross the river
Before winter's end!"

Failure

I began singing in the choir
At the wrong moment: out of fear, shame?
"Alright, get out!" said the teacher.
"Get out!"

I descended from the last row
Like a red pepper plucked from the beam,
And counted the steps, one by one,
To the end,
Under the earth
With the weight of one hundred eyes on my shoulders.

There Before the Tribes Arrived

You were
There before the tribes arrived
With your milk in a fissure in the rock
And with your feet in salt water.
They gave you but one name: Shkodra.

And they called you a crowned city
And they cast stones at your head
And ancient iron.

How often did you awaken drenched with blood
And observe yourself in the mirror?
Bearing a woman's name, you bathed in the waters
Of the river and enthroned yourself with fresh garments
Upon the cliff,
Your brow shining in the sun over the fields.

In the Shade of Things

In the shade this afternoon where I took my rest
I plucked a blade of grass in my thoughts.
The night crickets are chirping.

Near the hearth I hear the pods
Of ginestra
Bursting in my breast.

To a Modern Poet

Your road is good:
The Parcae are the ugliest faces
Of classical myths. You did not write of them,
But of stone slabs and of human brows
Covered in wrinkles, and of love.

Your verses are to be read in silence
And not before the microphone
Like those of other poets,

The heart
Though under seven layers of skin
Is ice,

Ice
Though under seven layers of skin.

That Mountain of Ice Divides Time

(That mountain of ice had a name,
Its name was taboo!)

Before my eyes closed in sleep,
I beheld that peak of pale ice
At my feet.
The wind arrived with the sun and melted it,
And there, in my shadow, appeared a flower.

Fragment

The worker sets off in search of work abroad
With a piece of sky in his arms
And sea salt in pinewood boxes.
In his hand he holds a slingshot,
And river pebbles in his mouth
Instead of bread.

The road before him is lit
By his eyes' glowing embers.

Two Generations

My father was
A sad-looking fellow,
A leafless olive tree
With black pits on every bough.

His words rumbled loudly
Within us
As if they were a famished wolf's howling
Alone in the barren cliffs.

My brother took
His place,
My barefoot brother
—cold wind on the horizon—

And blew at the autumnal fire
With full cheeks,
And all the sparks became
Sons.

Abandoned Village

Abandoned village
Behind the back of the earth
With houses and lanes which abut
Cliffs.

Inside, the old people light
Fires in the evening in ashes
Burned endlessly. The moon
After setting everywhere else,
Stops for a moment at their windows
And speaks to the folk
Frightened of the Evil Eye.

MARTIN CAMAJ

167

Hostile Sea

The sea bears everything with it, say the old people,
With the ever-blowing wind on one side
And pine and fruit trees on the other
Pressed to the ground.
We, the ancient inhabitants,
Love the land. Even the crickets
Bursting in the hot roots of the pine trees
Smell of resin and not of the sea.

Even the spirits of gods
Are hidden in the rocks and not in the salty
Sea! Sweet figs
Swoon red-lipped on their heads
In sacrifice.

Fragile Land

    to the tribes below the Drin

Between Molç Mountain and Qerret
There opens a gorge leading down to the river,
Formed as if it had been a lake,
And we were out there alone, on it, still,
In dugouts of maple.

We used to know by heart
The names of choice fish and not
Of preying birds and wild
Foliage.

Even the sheen in our eyes
Would be blue and not black.

We would float in the water
Not in the clouds.

KASËM TREBESHINA
1926–

Among the little-known figures of the early years of postwar Albanian literature is Kasëm Trebeshina. Trebeshina was born in Berat, in southern Albania, and studied at the Normal School (Shkolla Normale) in Elbasan until joining the Communist resistance movement in 1942. After World War II, he studied at the Ostrovsky Theatre Institute in Leningrad. A committed Communist, but by no means a conformist, Trebeshina left the party and later the Writers' Union in Tirana. Much of his work was written in the late 1940s and early 1950s, but never published. His opposition to the regime of Enver Hoxha caused him to vanish from the literary scene with scarcely a trace. After seventeen years in prison—a comparatively light sentence, as he later noted—and twenty years of silence, Trebeshina resurfaced in 1990 with a handful of other writers, artists, and intellectuals. His poetry and voluminous prose have been published in recent years, making him a respected, if not easy, figure of Albanian intellectual culture.

The Iceberg

An iceberg broke off in the Arctic,
It longed for and sought the Equator,
It voyaged afar through the oceans,
Day and night in the azure surge swimming.

Kissed by the waves, it was melting,
But ardor and lust burned within it,
The iceberg thus shortened its journey,
And melted to die in confusion.

We Met in the Darkness

The two of us met in the darkness
In the darkness we parted once more,
No words of farewell to each other,
Embarking and leaving the shore.

We vanished then into the shadows
Separated, yes, each went his way,
We bid a good-bye to the seacoast,
But no words to each other could say.

The Storks

Two storks soar over an island,
From the heights do they gaze in flight slow,
Beating wings both in grace and in grandeur,
O'er the cypress trees growing below.

Two storks fly over an island,
They ply the blue skies without rest,
In glory they circle and eye it,
Then continue their path to the West.

The Pelicans

In a pond are three pelicans paddling,
They're as white as the light in a dream,
Three pelicans gliding in splendor,
As they ponder the mist and its gleam.

In a pond are three pelicans searching
For a life they have not, ne'er will see,
For a place and a realm far beyond them,
For a space in a cosmos-to-be.

In a pond are three pelicans longing
For fish and themselves in the blue,
In a pond are three pelicans swimming,
As they conjure that cosmos untrue.

Evening

Night is falling,
Sinking, settling over towns,
Over fields,
Mountains,
And seas.

Falling, sinking for the living,
For the trees
And stones . . .

Falling, settling for the couple parting,
For the one who will die,
For the one to be born,
For all those who will meet again,
For a couple languishing in sighs
And silence,
Falling on the weary waves,
Sinking in this prison,
Falling, yes, for you,
Sinking, for me, too,
Falling, settling . . .

KASËM TREBESHINA

FATOS ARAPI
1930–

Fatos Arapi, from Zvërnec, near the port city of Vlora, is the author of philosophical verse, love lyrics, and poignant elegies on death. He studied economics in Sofia, Bulgaria, from 1949 to 1954 and worked in Tirana as a journalist and lecturer in modern Albanian literature. In his first two collections, *Poetic Paths* (*Shtigje poetike* [Tirana, 1962]) and *Poems and Verse* (*Poema dhe vjersha* [Tirana, 1966]), he made use of more modern verse forms than did his contemporaries and set the course for a renewal of Albanian poetry after years of stagnation.

Child of the Ionian Sea, Arapi has never lost his fascination with the sparkling waters of the Mediterranean, the tang of the salt air, and the intensity of light on the southern coast, all of which permeate his verse. His true poetic vocation can be glimpsed in the creation of an equilibrium between the harmony of the waves and the rhythmic impulses of his being. Arapi is the author of over twenty-five books. Since the fall of the Communist dictatorship in particular, he has published numerous volumes of verse and short stories, and he remains a leading figure of contemporary Albanian literature.

Leaving Vlora

I am leaving without saying good-bye to the sea.

  This one time
I did not foray to those familiar banks to bid farewell
To the gulls. I can no longer bear their absence.
Perhaps I am growing old,
My cells are beginning to falter and perhaps . . .
My heart is failing.
I can no longer stand
That distance of body from body.

Must I be off?
  Without turning back!

Yet on my lacerated lips
Do I sense the searing sting of iodine and sea salt.

You Will Come

You will come, my beloved, will you not?
Because you know I am waiting for you,
Listening to the heavy breath of evening,
Listening to the whisper of the wait,
Listening to the sigh of my solitude.
You will come, my beloved, will you not?
For you know that, if I could,
I would spin the planet
Like an orange in my hand,
To make time fly faster
    to have you with me at last. . . .

The Brothers of Pegasus

Ancient confusion in those wise,
    those fond eyes . . .
Beside a car, beneath a traffic light,
Elegant, glistening in the sun
    and the wind.
    They neigh,
The brothers of Pegasus. Volatile,
As if spewed from the bowels of the earth.
With dazzling tassels on their brows
    they snort,
The coursers of Kosova.

Poems on My Mother

Little Mother

Mother has shrunk,
As if constantly stooping,
My heart quivers,
So brittle, so tiny . . .
Almost as if she were my child,
    my mother.
She paces the room, back and forth,
Talks to herself,
Is always searching in a corner,
Has always lost something,
Something or other.
She paces the room, back and forth,
And I get the feeling
She is going to trip over
The beams of sunlight
Flooding through the window,
    my mother.

And Don't Forget

I just took her to the hospital
    and she says to me:
"When you come by tomorrow, bring me my slippers,
And the scissors for my nails,
And the newspaper.
O my little treasure, and don't forget
The black scarf,
    my widow's scarf."

No More Letters

I don't get any more letters from my mother,
Letters in which she always asks for money,

Money for her heart medication,
Money for her eye treatment.
My mother's eyes cannot see anymore,
My mother's heart does not beat anymore,
And now, at the end of every month
I have two hundred leks left over in my pocket.

To whom shall I send them?

Winter Sun

How quickly the flowers have covered my mother's grave,
February has just begun, and already the violets
And the daisies are everywhere,
This is my mother,
Like a winter sun
Down
There.

I Dislike Achilles

I dislike Achilles,
He's a looming threat, majestic
    and fatal,
With winged feet he comes and goes
In the pallid agony of Troy.
I mourn for his mother, Thetis,
The goddess of my sea.
But I detest Achilles,
His thundering wrath.
And I myself am Hector
With that cruel spear piercing my breast
At the Scaean Gates.

To budding mankind
I leave three sanguine words
Fatherland . . . Freedom . . . and from numbed lips,
    Andromache!

Where to Inter You?

With you in my arms, with you in my arms,
Dear and frigid, where to inter you?
Within my mind? You shunned that place,
Within my soul? It cannot be there.

I tread the earth, I traverse time,
But find no room, no tomb to inter you,
At last I return and enter a teardrop,
There I shall place you, lay you to rest.

Where Is That Old Man?

Where is that old man who used to sit
Over there, at the table near the window,
Frank as his posture,
Oblivious to his loneliness,
In front of a cup of coffee,
Plunged into eternal conversation with you?

With the smile of an ancient statue,
Though statues do not move from the spot,
He got up and departed,
Conscious like the wear and tear of time.

. . . conscious like fading light.

I Awaited the Nights, Standing

I awaited the nights, standing,
With flaming eye, I searched
    for the eye of darkness.

Back and forth, back and forth,
Left and right, left and right,
I was an abyss of oblivion
Filled only by you.
I awaited the nights, standing,
I told the minutes your name,
Told them again and again,
That they would know, would feel
What a broken heart is like,
What weeping is like,
The blind sorrow of separation,
And painful memory, what it all is like.

The rivers of time wanted to sleep,
I awaited the depths of night,
    standing.

The dawn of their passing
Shone on my brow.

And She Turned Up

She was in rapture,
Dancing,
As blithe as a tiny ray of light flitting through the darkness,
Thus she entered my tragic human
    fate.

FATOS ARAPI

Those Who Still Love

Those who have no food,
When they dream of food,
Let them think of you and me.
Those who have no fire,
When they dream of fire,
Let them think of you and me.
The insomniacs of this world
With their eyes wide open like the night,
In the depth of their nights,
Let them think of you and me.
Those who have perished
And who still love—
Let them think of you and me.

How Can I Endure the Autumn?

How can I endure the autumn
If my soul is autumn through and through?
The minutes swelled and October
Snuffed them out like candles.

Pale flame of the pyre,
In pain which is no longer even pain
I am a tomb and I alone know
What lies within me.

I Arose

I arose and left my grave.

In the darkness I sought you,
Holding a lamp.
In my hand,
Three bright daffodils.

Please, fill my eyes
With your smile.

It was for you I left my grave.

DRITËRO AGOLLI
1931–

Dritëro Agolli is a writer who has had a far from negligible influence on the course of contemporary literature. He was head of the Albanian Union of Writers and Artists from 1973 until 1992. Agolli was born to a peasant family in Menkulas, in the Devoll region near Korça, and finished secondary school in Gjirokastra in 1952. He later continued his studies at the Faculty of Arts of the University of Leningrad and took up journalism upon his return to Albania, working for the daily newspaper *Zëri i Popullit* (The People's Voice) for fifteen years. Besides his presidency of the Writers' Union from 1973 until his retirement on January 31, 1992, he also served as a deputy in the People's Assembly.

Agolli first attained success as a poet of the soil. His early verse collections introduced him to the reading public as a sincere and gifted lyric poet of the soil and demonstrated masterful verse technique. An attachment to his roots came to form the basis of his poetic credo. Agolli delights in earthy rhymes and unusual figures of speech. His fresh, clear, direct verse, colored with the warm foaming milk of brown cows in the agricultural cooperatives, with ears of ripening corn in the Devoll valley, and with the dark furrows of tilled soil, lost none of the bucolic focus that remained the poet's strength and which he cultivated consciously.

The Cow

The cow chews her cud in the hay-filled barn,
I lean my face against her great flank
Feeling from her inner depths the warmth,
The warmth of hay gathered in the meadows.
Over her black horns hangs an electric light
Shining down into the pail of milk.
I cannot leave the cow.
With my face against her flank, I smell the foaming milk.
The milkmaid gently removes the pail
And waits a moment, her hands dripping.
She says:
    "Are you a vet?"
I lift my face from the cow:
    "No, a poet."
She smiles and studies me with her blue eyes,
Lovely, wise, and peaceful.
She reflects for a while and realizes
I cannot write a line without a cow. . . .

The Wind

In the wind the trees cower and huddle together,
In the wind the trees long for a warming embrace,
But what of the two of us,
Far from each other?
I know not what wind could unite us apace.

The Snow

I remember the words that my grandfather spoke,
When we went for a walk in the white, silent snow:
The snow stays so quiet while icy and living,
It only speaks out in its ultimate woe.

On the Appeal of Poetry

You say that I've written too much about cows,
And of grain in the fields I have penned too much verse.
So what? You have butter and milk in the morning,
At supper there's always that little white roll
On your plate, and beside it you clamor for meat.

You assert that we lose some poetic excitement
When mentioning cows all the time in our verse,
The appeal of a poem, you say is not from pastures,
But rather when under our skin a line bursts
With words, you insist, from some lofty preserve.

Yet listen, I've never, as much as I wanted,
Gone on about cows, yes, they merit much more,
I can't sever them from my pen and my paper,
It's cows that inspire me, my spring and my fall,
I would, if I could, teach them how to write poems.

I'm sure they'd be better than most of our bards!

The Moon over the Meadow

Like a title the moon hovers over the meadow,
Like a title that rises from a poem of love,
And in such a fair meadow did I once stand waiting,
I patiently hoped that you'd come with me, too. . . .

This evening I watch it in that tranquil meadow,
Observe as it sets in the wet dewy grass,
And ask myself, plunged both in thought and in wonder,
How oft has that title been penned and erased?

DRITËRO AGOLLI

181
▾

How oft has it been written and razed do I ponder,
Much as the titles have changed in my verse.
And through my gray hair does the wind blow and skitter,
As love, now departed, is flitting elsewhere.

Simple but Useful Things

A cane, be it smooth, be it bumpy and knotty,
Some use for a blind man it always accords,
It's good for the lame, burdened down by their journey,
And handy for folk when attacked by the hordes.

A cane, be it smooth, be it bumpy and knotty,
Is worthy to wield both outside and at home,
At home to protect you against wrathful neighbors,
Outside to ward off mangy mad dogs who roam.

A cane in appearance could be fair or be ugly,
It's useful indeed for some other events,
You need it to beat all the dust from your handbags,
Or knock on the door when no buzzer presents.

A cane is a requisite for a policeman,
Is prized by a warden in prison cells damp,
A cane was once held by Apostle Saint Peter,
And once by blind Homer deprived of a lamp.

The Secrets of the Candle

The candle has something quite secret about it,
An aspect you cannot that well comprehend,
With its wax do hot tears form and flow down the taper,
As you sit still observing that saintly stick's end.

The candle breathes out mystic wonder and goodness,
Takes hold and possesses your being again,
To dreams from the Bible you then are transported,
And all of life's vanities wither and wane.

In the drips of the candlestick holder's hot tallow,
Ensconcing your father's pale eyes which draw near,
Buzuku arrives, Budi, Bardhi, Bogdani,
Naim's there before you and melts in his tear.

You're touched and consoled like a saint come from ashes,
With the charred row of years stretching back for an age,
You sit there in silence and wait for the candle,
To speak and instruct you like some distant sage.

DIN MEHMETI
1932–

Din Mehmeti is among the best-known classical representatives of
contemporary verse in Kosova. He was born in 1932 in the village
of Gjocaj i Junikut, near Gjakova, and studied Albanian language
and literature at the University of Belgrade. He later lectured at the
teacher-training college in Gjakova. Although he has published
some prose, literary criticism, and a play, he is known primarily for
his figurative poetry, which appeared in fifteen volumes between
1961 and 1999.

Mehmeti's verse is one of indigenous sensitivity. He relies on
many of the figures, metaphors, and symbols of northern Albanian
popular verse to imbue and stabilize his restless lyrics with the stoic
vision of the mountain tribes. The creative assimilation of folklore
remains strongly fused with a realist current, at times ironic, which
takes its roots in part from the ethics of revolt in the tradition of
Migjeni and Esad Mekuli. Mehmeti's poetic restlessness is, none-
theless, not focused on messianic protest or social criticism but on
artistic creativity and individual perfection.

I Have One Request

I have one request
That will turn a stone into an apple,
An apple into a bird,
When the star learns its name,
It will vanish in a smoke puff.

A tearful request
That will turn the bird into a bullet,
The bullet into a flower,
Grave upon grave
Until a whole hillside sprouts.

It is the sigh of the soul
That burns in song
And is born in its own death.

Let us amass the bones, it says,
And form a tower of love
For the future will demand of us
A lighthouse to face the storm.

Self-Portrait

I am a sky gnawed
By the fog,
A wind tormenting the trees.

I shall not surrender to my fate.

Everything that has befallen,
The birds charred to ashes,
Is mirrored
In my soul.

I shall not surrender to my fate.

I have seen my legend
Dripping blood
And have found my tomb in the sun,
My flaming abyss.

I shall not surrender to my fate.

I am everything which has crumbled,
Only to rise
In forest clearings
Named after bolts of lightning.

Mourning erodes me with its laughter,
Screaming with its song.

I shall not surrender to my fate.

Night of the Poets

When silence envelops all things,
When everyone is asleep,
Do poets awaken
To seethe in their verse,

To squeeze from it
The bitter blood of thought,

Their spirits—a battlefield,
In the fever of words
They perish slowly with no cry.

A Legend

A legend,
A word which never withers,
Is a light pursued by darkness
In the accursed canyons
Which proclaims judgment on its own wisdom.

A legend—it is my people
Seared like a stone burst into flame
And yet green like the buds of first blossoms,
Fled like the ray which slipped into the abyss,
Come like the last soldier with victory on his flag,
Bound in a root enshrouded by earth
Where fear grows moldy in the marrow of crags,
Dreaming of snowdrifts.

A legend,
A smoky fortress,
Amidst the storms of time,
The meadows of hope,
Advancing through my verse.

Swollen Roads

Swollen roads of a ceremonial square,
They don't even bid each other farewell.

In the rays of the sun
Can be heard
The clang of old swords.

And lament deceives joy,
And death deceives life.

The ghosts of Macbeth,
The wrathful wood,

An unyielding tumult
Is about to set forth.

I have nowhere to go beyond my blood,
I have nowhere to go beyond my tongue.

We will bond to the girth of the earth,
As a mad dog is chained to its hut. . . .

My Sailboat

Speed o'er the waves, sailboat of mine,
Conquer the sea and vanquish fear.

Sail to the foaming banks
Where wounds are healed.

The sea is as deep as blood's victories.

Pluck the blue from the sky,
Put trowels to these wrinkles,
And, on seagulls' wings,
Make the dawn a nest.

Sailboat of mine, sorrow of my journey,
Orphaned children we are, you and I.

Should we perish somewhere far away,
Only the winds will mourn us.

Speed o'er the waves, heart of fire,
For my life and yours are elusive and blithe. . . .

DIN MEHMETI

The Past

Gory revenge wrought in the dark,
Without a song or a cry.
The lust for blood
Turned you to wretched stone
Long before my birth.

May every pierced slab know that name,
Buried in every mother's bosom,
Your calamity,
Black beast. . . .

MIHAL HANXHARI
1930–1999

Mihal Hanxhari was born in Kentucky, in the United States, where his father emigrated in 1907. In 1931, the family returned to Albania and settled in Tirana. Hanxhari began writing and publishing short stories during secondary school. He studied history and geography in Budapest and, after graduation in 1954, returned to Albania to teach secondary school in Korça and Tirana. In 1960, he was appointed director of the library at the University of Tirana, a job that gave him rare access to the world of literature and literary culture. He was fired from this job for political reasons in 1975, denounced as a liberal and a spreader of bourgeois culture, and was transferred to a modest post at a local library branch, where he worked until 1990. From 1993 to 1995, he taught Albanian at l'École des Langues Orientales, in Paris. He died on June 3, 1999.

Only since his death has Hanxhari been discovered as a writer. His poetic world, now greatly admired, is unusual in Albanian literature. We find in him the reminiscence of Cavafy and poignant glimpses of nature not unlike those in Japanese haiku. He would seem to have been entirely uninfluenced by the heavy-handed doctrine of socialist realism that held sway in Albania until 1990. Hanxhari published nothing during his lifetime.

Night of Stillness

Night of stillness,
A faint rustling of stars
Can be heard
As they blaze in the heavens.
Under the broken bridge
The sluggish river bears away
An unraveled wreath
Cast by the moon onto the water
For the soul of the wounded bridge.

A Severed Prayer

The broken bridge,
Two fractured limbs
Hover over the river,
Two arms outstretched,
Silent and numb,
Which cannot
Link hands
For a long prayer
Severed in the middle.

Petals

A spring night
And rain outside
Bathes the plum blossoms in the garden,
Drenches the lemon blossoms on the balcony,
Soaks the solemn, empty streets,
And, in a corner of my soul,
So many petals settle on the water.

Leaves

I know, I know,
It is not springtime
That will remember the leaves,
It is the leaves that will remember
The springtime
Someday.

The Linden Trees

In the wee hours, the fragrance of the linden trees,
Sweet venom, enraptures me.
The streets are empty, lights in windows wink out,
The stars appear to have breathed that aroma,
They, too, are drunk with delight.
All are fast asleep,
And night, a great owl spreading its wings,
Abandons the gloomy rafters of a rooftop,
And, gliding soundless,
Alights on a nearby wall.
The two of us watch in silence.

The Earth

The wind whisked away the clouds,
The deluge stopped, the sun has peeked out,
The last raindrops plop from the leaves,
And the earth, parched and dying of thirst,
Slurps and drinks its fill.

The Storm

With the storm passed, clouds gone, night calmed,
The scattered stars have reappeared,
And in the old plane tree,
Amidst its leafless branches,
The Big Dipper, flung by the wind,
Is stuck like a child's balloon.

The Cypress Trees

O moon,
Distant sister, dead sister,
They are felling, are scything
The cypress trees.

While on Its Way

I thought of you while spring was on its way,
In every raindrop none but you I pondered,
In every budding leaf you came to mind,
I thought of you in every petal blooming,
I thought of you in every petal falling,

I thought of you upon those azure evenings
When air grew damp in undetected flowers,
When from behind the walls of old-time gardens
The numbing fragrance spread of ancient loves,
I thought of you on sleepless nights, eyes open,
When hands of trees poured stars into my window,
And wide awake, I thought of you 'til morning,
O night so long, you knew what I was thinking,

I thought of you while spring was on its way,
As clouds themselves on mountain crests do wonder,
As lilies open slowly in the nighttime.
My soul has now become a flow'ring lily,
And spring has entered it and found you there.

Voiceless

Like a tattoo on a shoulder,
Like a scar from coals on flesh,

Like a statue's fractured forearm,
Like cold marble's faults and cracks,

Like marks which never vanish,
Like mute pain we are to each other.

To Sleep

How can you doze
And not be aware
Of the gentle fragrance that wills you to sleep,
Like white petals floating
Down a river?

Without You

I long to be the liquid that your lips drink,
—you are the fragrance of every flower I love,
I long to be the slumber on your brow when you sleep,
—you draw near me in my dreams like a shadow at night,

Why such sorrow in your eyes?
—how can I die alone without you?

Rapture

We did not drink that night,
But we bought so many carnations,
We flung them on our bed
And on the blossoms our immaculate bodies.

We did not forget that June night,
Oh, the memory of it rends my heart like a knife.

Unquenchable Fire

Fall has come, the fog has fallen,
I walk the streets with an unseen pyre,
On my lips remain your kisses,
I pace the lanes with unquenchable fire.

Lemon Blossoms

You once struck me with lemon blossoms,
And the moon bewitched me with their fragrance.

You once gave me your blood as a flower,
And I wept over you.

You once left me alone, eyes closed,
And, blind now, I find you no more.

MIHAL HANXHARI

Where Is

When the window was like a sun
And in that shady room, summer came in from the garden,
And you lounging, your blouse undone,
With nipples, burnt clay-colored,
And the clock counted the passing of our lives,
Where is that afternoon
That has lingered in my memory, lounging
Like an Etruscan terra-cotta?

AZEM SHKRELI
1938–1997

Azem Shkreli is a central figure of modern Albanian poetry in Kosova. He was born in the village of Shkrel, in the Rugova highlands near Peja. After elementary education in the village of Nakëll, he attended secondary school in Prishtina, from which he graduated in 1961. He went on to study at the University in Prishtina and graduated in 1965 with a diploma in Albanian language and literature. From 1960 to 1975, Shkreli was director of the People's Provincial Theater (Teatri Popullor Krahinor) in Prishtina. For a time, he was also a member of the executive board of the Writers' Union of Yugoslavia. In 1975, he became director of the film studio Kosovafilm, a post he held until he was expelled by the Serb administration in 1991. He was then forced into exile and lived on and off in Germany for several years. He died at Prishtina airport on a visit to his homeland.

Although Shkreli also wrote short stories and plays, he remained primarily a poet throughout his life. He published a total of ten verse collections from 1960 to 1997. His works have had an influence on almost all Kosovar poets of the younger generation. His verse has been translated into English in *Blood of the Quill*.

Before the Elegy

One day you will press to your bosom
The fallen leaves of your seasons
And will search for yourself in vain
On the forgotten pathways of a generation.
No longer will you have hair woven by the wind
Or rainbow vision to measure the beginning
And the end of your short deceit.
One day you will expose your age
Like the dowry of a dead bride
And will count the defunct butterflies
Of dispersed dawns
And you will have no more fire on your lips,
No more tears in your warm smiling eyes,
You will weep falsely and astonish
The young men.

One day you will bite your lips.
You will spit on your footprints
And will baptize each dusk
With one repentance that pains.
No longer will you have those sea-blue eyes
Or the graceful pace of the deer
To see how the blossoms ridicule you
And to run from your own shadow.

Beware, my dear, for the loveliest girls
Are slain by their own beauty.

With Migjeni

I raise your mighty fist to strike
The scarlet skeleton of autumn, like
An echo, I see it—each time I rend
A dead branch off our season's end.

AZEM SHKRELI

I raise your mighty fist to flail
Fall's frail skeleton, frigid and pale,
And each time my forlorn desires' stone
Strikes my fortress forehead's bone.

I raise your mighty fist to crush, to tear
Fall's sick skeleton o'er the peaks, us, in the air,
But my breath and my words knot my rage in vain,
Someone is weeping. Fall or pain?

Over Europe

Evening. We are in flight, plucking at the wool
Of the clouds. Beneath us a white kingdom,
Azure triumph. We speed on and pay no heed,
Past frontiers, armies, flocks,

As if atop the century, and below us
The musty stench of history and wars as if they had not been.
A lady stifles a sigh in her handkerchief
Somewhere over Mauthausen.

I look out the window. I do not know why I laugh
While slowly emptying a bottle with my friend.
Who will be born down below us tonight?
Merchants? Sartre? Generals?
Evening. We are in flight. Below us pensive
Europe drowses and droops over ponderous affairs,
Sleep on, wise lady, I never aspired
To your tastes, your whims which were not mine.

The Death of the Highlander

Bow not a single head,
For you will topple his oak trees.

Mourn not, be hard as stone,
For you will cause his peaks to crumble.

No tears, not one,
For you will dry up his springs.

In his eyes only
The daylight forgot to recede.

What a gloomy thought,
What a chilling thought beneath all brows.

Lucky him. What a death!

Obituary for a Bird

It gave azure freedom to its venture,
Feathers drenched in sun and light,
Who knows what words its beak was writing
Or if yearning drove its flight.

Perhaps it broke the vault of noonday
Westward banked, left wing askew,
Heat dripped of blood, sipped the Aegean,
Black was the bird, or fatally it flew.

Monument to Mic Sokoli

On Europe falls the snow,
Blankets many a Bismarck's hair,
Gunshots, guilty banners billow
In forgetting, planted there

From the past, a cannonball
Discharges a painful din,
Blood burgeons, a crimson pall,
The epic of my kin.

A Tale About Us

The prime of life
We ate as an unripe fruit

On the branch remained only
The bird's voice and feathers

Summer passed and drank
All its own red wine

One got drunk, another
Fell on the horn of a goat

Another clambered onto its stubborn head
To see what time it was

The wisest one beseeched God and
The devil not to pray for us.

The Toast

On the third day they slaughtered lambs, thrust
The cold knife into whiteness and grass

And the lymph fell upon butterbur and they drank and cursed
They swilled and swore at the skies

And at the head of the table the divine devils of wine
Blew on the goat horn and the world slept

On the third day they slaughtered lambs and imbibed
From the milky pallor, the whole day was bleeding.

Frightened Light

Something must be written in black
For the seas are not in vain, not futile
The ravens, the worms, the gods and the nights,
Something must be written, pleasing is the gleam
Of frightened ink, the dumbstruck
Is femininely fair, something must be
Written, it is the only somber light
Not spit at by the devil, the only woman
Not shamefully stripped bare, not fruitlessly
Do fires and martyrs envy her aura.
Should we flee the omens tonight?
Should they not chastise us with eternal ruth?
Bend down, enraged beauty, let us sip
Of your cup, to hell with it all,
For something must be written in black.

Anathema

Because I had ancient sand, archaic dew
In my eyebrows, wine in the throat of my bird and because
One and one are two, like two guns, two women,
Two white stones above the head of every wise man,
Because there was no wound on this side of the river,
There were bridges, healing herbs and peace, and because
I kissed the luscious earth with my thick neolithic lips,
Because I got my reed pipe out of hell and played it
To my light, scaring the clouds and crows away, because
I early sowed my shadow in the sun, and because
I had fire on my spear, rye in my hair, and strands of gray
On churches, on ages, on graves,
Because I had blood, and my leaf flute had language, they
      damned me.

Wolf's Spoor

Where did it come from
In howling and hunger?

Barefoot in the night it slunk
Through the darkness, under tables

It thrust its big black claws
Into the peace and calm,

Through their chains the dogs crunched
And lunged at the stake,

People's hands and eyes and steps
Grew wide in wonder,

Last night in our front yards
A wolf skulked, its spoor among us.

Departure of the Migrants

Farewell in shoulder bags, farewell in the air,
In eyes farewell.
Time is being split into two, the sad hour hovers
Overhead like a huge axe,
Sweat-soaked bodies of wives, young in years,
Sighs of mothers. Wait for us,
Let the plants and the children grow, let the thirst take
The bird and the voice and the salt.
Let only the roads get older, let their hair grow white
At our departure, not at our return.
You black road, you long snake, you consumed us,
You chased us beyond oblivion.

Martin's Stone

for Martin Camaj

Friend of the blood of the quill, for years
As a child I searched for you with "A Flute in the Mountains,"
Who knows that you raised me in the peaks among the stones
With a word chisel?

And today in Bavaria after so much time away
I come across a stone from Dukagjini
Raised on bone milk from mother earth,
I am Martin's Stone.

Leave me a while, leave me, Martin's Stone,
That I take you arm in arm, as once in the highlands,
That I cool the coals of longing and emigration
And then I will be gone, I will not stay.

For this land of ours wants
Its stones and poets scattered around the world,
We are not in mourning, yet may the pain
At Martin's Stone never be in vain.

Song of Shame

Tonight
I wept for you tonight
Arberia

I am not ashamed
That I shed tears
I feel distressed that there was
Nothing more I could do

I wept of shame.

ALI PODRIMJA
1942–

Ali Podrimja was born in Gjakova, at the foot of the so-called Accursed Mountains. After a difficult childhood, he studied Albanian language and literature in Prishtina. Author of over a dozen volumes of cogent and assertive verse since 1961, he is recognized both in Kosova and in Albania itself as a leading and innovative poet. Indeed, he is considered by many to be the most typical representative of modern Albanian verse in Kosova and is certainly the Kosovar poet with the widest international reputation.

In the early 1980s, he published the masterful collection *Lum Lumi* (Prishtina, 1982), which marked a turning point not only in his own work but also in contemporary Kosovar verse as a whole. This immortal tribute to the poet's young son Lumi, who died of cancer, introduced an existentialist preoccupation with the dilemma of being, with elements of solitude, fear, death, and fate. Podrimja is nonetheless a laconic poet. His verse is compact in structure, and his imagery is direct, terse, and devoid of any artificial verbosity. Every word counts. What fascinates the Albanian reader is his compelling ability to adorn this elliptical rocky landscape, reminiscent of Albanian folk verse, with unusual metaphors, unexpected syntactic structures, and subtle rhymes.

Ghazal

My salvation
Your body, O woman—
A verdant meadow.

My health
Your body, O woman—
Scorching noon on a branch.

My hatred
Your body, O woman—
Evening fallen on its knees.

O woman, O woman, deep sea.

The Illness of My Family

for my father, Hamzë Podrimja

My father God bless him died of a stomach ulcer
Before having his say about Love and Mankind
My mother God bless her thrice was operated on in the Hospital
Thrice the Wolf howled around our house
A tumor in my brother burst into madness
He gave up the ghost beside a fountain when no one was watching

My sister we buried three meters deep
In the shade of a poplar we buried her one summer's evening
With all the pus of a filthy world
I, I shall wander a planet drowned in dreams
Farther and farther I shall flee from the blood and the self
If my nerves are altered in the tambourine of time
O illness of my family
Confounded game
Of fate.

The Dead Clock

The clock stopped
Just as I was counting the strokes

Time was emptied of Movement
Breathing
And Me.

My room lost its balance
The members changing their form
Dreams creeping through the hands

I called the Repairman came
Screw upon screw
He changed

To make the clock time-tight

I did what I could to revive it
To have the walls return to the room
And Movement and Breathing

Look under the old family photo
It stands silent
Nailed to the air.

And You Dead

It was summer
Overhead the sun
Shadows, you around Europe

From that horrible journey
You returned one day with eyes wide open
You entered your father's poem without knocking

There you are in safety Lumi
I swear no harm
Will come to you

It was summer
The sun in the west
And you dead, earth.

Death Was Quicker

You were far away so far away Lumi
My feet fell off my elbows dripped in blood
    as I followed you

Now you are far away so far away
Death was quicker than I was.

The Meadow

Somewhere over there was our house
    Grandfather's Wall and father's Poplar Tree
    The Stakes surrounding a red space

ALI PODRIMJA

205
▾

Somewhere over there we used to go down
　　To the Dukagjin Fountain to quench our thirst
　　To eat bread and salt with the gods of Mount Pashtrik

Under the scythe the grass has now grown
　　And we collect the fallen teeth of the wolf
　　among the kernels in the blade
　　Grandfather's Wall and father's Poplar Tree
　　And the Stakes waft through my memory

With my hands in my pockets I end the day
　　Collapsing into unraveled space
　　And listening to the wild neighing of foamy-white horses
　　Until late at night

Over there in the meadow where our house once stood.

It Is the Albanian's Fault

It is the Albanian's fault
That he breathes
And walks on two legs

That I take tranquilizers
And swat flies all day
In the Toilet

It is the Albanian's fault
That he besmirches his own wife
And frightens my family

That my hand cannot reach the apple
On the highest branch
That he has filled the Well with dead words

It is the Albanian's fault
That not more of Turkey exists,
More of America, of Norway

That the Gulag is so far away

That they chose me and sent me
To sniff him out
Does death smell

It is all the more the Albanian's fault
That he does not eat
Or close his eyes and sleep

That our sewers are broken
And the Catacombs of the Balkans
Have fallen into ruins

It is the Albanian's fault
That he whiles away the time under the moon
And breaks windows and stirs up muddy water

That he speaks Albanian that he eats Albanian
    that he shits Albanian

It is the Albanian's fault
The Albanian is the one at fault
For all my undoings

Both for my broken tooth
And for my frozen smile
So therefore: BULLET

Ha ha ha
Ha ha
Ha

May God have mercy!

If

If a people
Have no poets
And no poetry of their own
For a National Anthology
Then treachery and barking
Will do the trick.

Who Will Slay the Wolf

for Francesco Altimari

And the gentleman said

Should you happen to come upon
An Albanian and a wolf
Slay the Albanian

When the Albanian heard the saying
He smiled
And rolled himself a cigarette

If you slay me
    my poor friend
Who will slay
The wolf

Poor herds.

A Child Is Dying in the Cellar

I shall go down there
    with a torch in my hand

A child is dying in the cellar
    is Mankind listening

Bread and Salt we shall divide among ourselves

The filthy hands the icy feet
    the bluish body
I shall fold into my arms

I shall breathe upon it and wrap it in prayers

In the cellar the hero of my century is dying

I shall go down there
    with a torch in my hand

And frequent the mice the darkness the spirits
My little friend is dying
    Is Mankind listening?

And the false deities argue
As to who has the most space
    for the grave.

The Albanians

God gave them nothing, not even grass
Only snakes
And stones

But they did have something
Which the Almighty never discovered
They lived long

ALI PODRIMJA

209
▾

And when they died
They died
Chanting *oi oi oi*

At each of their heads
Fell
A plane tree split in two.

Or Rather

Should you long
     to see Albanians
Go down to the train station in a big city

Worn-out shoes they wear
And white socks

Or rather

On Marienplatz or at the Eiffel Tower
     just whistle a heroic tune
Into a circle you go
     there you have them all those rigid faces

But do not be frightened off
For solitude can make you sick
That awesome brutality of cement.

XHEVAHIR SPAHIU
1945–

Xhevahir Spahiu is one of the most forceful and vociferous poets
of modern Albania, a voice of survival. He comes from the central
Albanian region of Skrapar, at the foot of lofty Mount Tomorr, the
legendary Father Tomorr of Albanian mythology. During the 1973

Purge of the Liberals, dictator Enver Hoxha referred to Spahiu by name for having composed the poem "Jetë" (Life). This poem contains the lines "Jam ai se s'kam qenë, do të jem ai që nuk jam" (I am who I have not been, I shall be who I am not), reminiscent, though by pure coincidence, of a line by French philosopher Jean-Paul Sartre. Although the poet had never had the opportunity of enjoying the forbidden fruits of the late French philosopher (as had the Albanian dictator obviously), he was condemned as an existentialist, which was tantamount to high treason. He survived only by the skin of his teeth, by channeling his passions into appropriate revolutionary fervor. After a few years he was allowed to publish once again. Now that the red tide has receded, Spahiu goes about his poet's business and is quite content to do so.

Among Spahiu's more recent verse collections are *Hellparadise* (*Ferrparajsa* [Elbasan, 1994]), *Hover* (*Pezull* [Elbasan, 1996]), and *The Danger* (*Rreziku* [Tirana, 2003]).

To Be with You

To touch your silence as one feels an object,
To stare deep into those eyes,
Where love drifts like a boat
And not to want to be with you forever?

To walk with my arm around your shoulders
And not to sense the roar of the blue waves,
Lemon trees over my head?
Boats like fires in the night?

To be with you,
To laugh with you,
And not to understand that the sea
Is trying to escape its own shell?

To be with you?
To be with you!

XHEVAHIR SPAHIU

In the Roots of Words

to the memory of Professor Eqrem Çabej

Words older than the *Iliad,*
Words younger than the sprouting twigs
Totter,
Are shrouded for a moment in haze.

He has left us . . .

He descended in silence to the bones of the earth
Where our language and molten lava have their source.

He is no longer . . .

He went to hew a house forever
In the roots of words.

Speech

They said to speech: you are now free.
But speech lacked the strength to reply: I've no need.
What use is it now
Since I did not speak out when I should have?
I am left without wings,
I am left without a sky,
I am life without a dream,
I am a dream without a life.
They said to speech: you are free.
It's hard, said speech, hard
To believe you're free.
When you've swallowed your own syllables,
When you've been slashed to a stump,
Even freedom becomes a prison.
They said to speech: freedom lives.

Speech replied:
I am not Constantine who set out seeking death.
They said to speech: you are freedom.
It doesn't take much to understand that.
Speech believed them
And opened its mouth,
Uttering
Not sounds,
  but blood.

To Wake Up Late

To wake up late means
Finding the flowers dewless, heads a-drooping.
To wake up late means
Love has left behind a pale imprint.
To wake up late means
Death has long signed your papers.

But wake up anyway.

Sketch

The Lombardy poplars spend their winter
Under a gray-leaden sky,
No more birds,
No more winds,
Here and there in them
Nests
Like wounds.

Translation of the River

I sit and translate the river,
Hard to render
This watery thing,
Rare words,
Fixed expressions,
Eternal rhythms,
A hundred fountains in unison
Recounted ancient myth.
All night long I translated the river.
At dawn
My version was gone.

Our History

The blade of the sword we came down in a dash.
The sword then came down upon us in a flash.

Kosova

The peasants in my part of the country asked me about Kosova.

River Drin, River Osum,
Mount Sharr, Mount Tomorr,
Here and there the same words spoken.

One difference is certain:
The shackles.

Torquemada

Chop off their heads, ordered Torquemada.
Without a trial? stammered a gray-haired judge.

God will be their judge, said the inquisitor,
Even those gone before them know that.

God himself turned gray,

Waiting in vain for the indictment.

EQREM BASHA
1948–

Eqrem Basha is among the most respected contemporary writers of
Kosova. He was born in Dibra, in the western, Albanian-speaking
region of what is now the Republic of Macedonia, but his life and
literary production are intimately linked to Kosova and its capital,
Prishtina, where he has lived and worked for the past three decades.
In the early 1970s, during the only real years of freedom in Kosova,
Basha moved to Prishtina to study language and literature at the
newly created Albanian-language university there. He later worked
for Prishtina television as editor of the drama section but was fired for
political reasons during the Serb takeover of the media in 1989 and
1990. Basha is the author of eight volumes of innovative verse span-
ning the years from 1971 to 1995, three volumes of short stories, and
numerous translations (in particular French literature and drama).
He is currently working in the publishing industry in Prishtina.

Basha is an enigmatic poet. Perplexing, fascinating, and difficult
to classify in a literary sense, he succeeds in transmitting a certain
mystique to the inquisitive reader. At one moment he seems coolly
logical and shows an admirable ability to reason deductively, and the
next moment he is overcome by absurd flights of fancy into a sur-
realistic world where apparently nothing makes any sense. His verse

is light, colloquial, and much less declamatory than that of many of his predecessors.

Nighttime Traveler of This World

He did not get up like everyone else—in the morning
For him the day began in the trenches of the desperate
He arrived in this world from the night
And travels nocturnally to reach the day's end

He did not get up when the sun rose
Nor was he born when ants awakened
In the final analysis you cannot write poetry about him
Because he is not human but a mole feeding
On the rotting roots of this world
He is neither alone nor with friends
To do his portrait you need shadows
Grayish hues and light filtering in through the fog

He did not get up like everyone else—in the morning
He travels his whole life long from the edge
To the heart of darkness

He belongs—as they say—to the family of the mole
Which *respectable* folk chase with poison
To protect their healthy roots

You cannot write even a verse about him
Although he is sensitive and employed
Married to a wife who loves him, with two or three children
With two or three mortgages and an apartment
In the third district of the second residential zone
Of Local Municipality No. 1 in Region No. 3

And yet—he is sensitive
He twice attempted to commit suicide
The third time no one noticed
He stopped in the middle of the road
And did not go through with it
For a beautiful day dawned, startled him and frightened him off

He did not get up like everyone else
Nor has he ever washed his face in the morning dew
The light reflecting in the sparkling waters of the pristine well
Always keeps him blind
This is why he does not sleep when the rest of us do
He does not get up when everyone else does
He is quite prosaic on matters of poetry
You cannot write a ballad, modern verse,
Or short lyrics about him
He is someone you never notice
From Building No. 7 of District No. 3, Unit CX 12/7, No. 23
On the 12th floor of Residence 47, left wing
A proletarian with a milk bottle at the door every day
And a roll of newspapers criticizing the degenerate morals
Of the world in which he lives

Any verse about him would be without appeal
And yet
He lives in this world
And merits
Having two or three words
Written about him
In a poem.

Cold

Two headlights
Two policemen
Keeping watch over the cold night

A bird
Killed in an accident
Lies in the frigid night
No dreams
No solemn funeral

I stand on its behalf
In the middle of the road
In the frozen night
And search
For a model obituary.

Balkan Menu

Don't set the table, love
Let's go out for dinner
We'll leave early
And come back late
Life here in Europe's changed
Come on, love, let's go
Let's have some punch
At the Admiral Bar
And a *coupe royale*
At the Montreal sidewalk café
In Benny's pool room
We'll try a carom behind our backs
We'll have a cappuccino
At Marilyn's cafeteria
And a martini with olives at the Florida Club
Don't set the table, love
Let's go out for dinner
To the Miami Pizzeria
And have a pizza New Jersey
An *escaloppe viennese* at the Roma restaurant
And then go to Parma's
For a *coupe macédonienne*

And when it gets late
We'll go back home
To empty our bowels
In a Balkan latrine.

The Street Sweepers of Prishtina

Who could know the town better
With the sandaled feet of children
On tank tracks

With the mouths of little boys
Drinking water
From tear gas cartridges?

Who could know the town better
Than those who wash it at night
And cannot cleanse its wounds?

No one
More than the clotted veins
Which turn pale in the morning
In the eternally busy vaults
Of Europe's morgue.

The Wolf

In the wilds of the forest
I saw only squirrels
Hares
Deer
Badgers

In the wilds of the forest
The wolf is always right beside you
He is your neighbor
You can smell him

In his jaws
Are pieces of your life.

The Nightingale Sings

Who is that bird singing on a branch alone
And where is its flock?

Which is the plaintive song
And which is the season?

    That bird has a voice adept
    At singing on a solitary branch
    No friends no family
    It has come to earth on its own
    With a flute in its beak and anguish
    Which is neither a wound
    Nor a song

What is that mourning so near which belongs to us?
Sing to us nightingale sing

The Audience

The head of the protocol department asked
What are you involved in
We are tired I said
Alright, but what are you involved in

In ourselves
We said
We have been occupied
We would like to have a little rest

Are you involved in politics
Oh, no
Our goal is freedom

The department head took note
And gave us a startled look

They look naive he said
As he came in to meet us
And desperate
They are Albanians
They come from a land of hatred
They want to be understood
They don't insist on love.

SABRI HAMITI
1950–

Born in Dumnica, near Podujeva, in Kosova, poet and critic Sabri
Hamiti studied comparative literature both in Zagreb and at l'École
Pratique des Hautes Études, in Paris, where the demigods of French
structuralism brought their influence to bear on him. He received his
doctorate from the University of Prishtina. Hamiti is the author of
numerous volumes of prose, poetry, and drama, as well as innovative
criticism. Among his most recent verse collections are *Knife of Oblivion* (*Thikë harrimi* [Prishtina, 1975]), *The Illyrian Stock* (*Trungu ilir*
[Prishtina, 1979]), *Identity Papers* (*Leja e njohtimit* [Prishtina, 1985]),
Chaosmos (*Kaosmos* [Prishtina, 1990]), and *ABC* (Prishtina, 1994).

The Telegram

You're off in Europe and we don't know where you are stop
You turned twenty-eight today stop
And Mirani turned eight stop
He's learned the whole alphabet stop
Last night he did all his homework stop
Penning it carefully in his notebook stop
Father bought some groceries stop
He's coughing again stop
Mother died three days ago stop
We buried her under the blooming hawthorn tree stop
We did not call you, did not know how stop
You're off in Europe and we don't know where you are stop
The hodja said the funeral could not be delayed stop
We did not eat cake for your birthday without you stop
The candles are burning and going out stop
Come back alive for we are still waiting stop
Stop stop stop.

The Telephone

He doesn't know how to read and write,
But he knows numbers up to ten,
Counting on his fingers.
Himself at one end of the line,
The world at the other,
He learned to talk.

Hello, hellooo!
He can call by heart
With his eyes closed.

Hello, hellooo!
This is number 1234567890.
Can I talk to the World?
Where is the World?

He doesn't know how to touch or feel,
Colors, faces, and scenes
He draws with words.

Hello, hellooo! . . . Telephoning
The world
Ahhh . . .

The world has fallen asleep
The telephone is dead.
His neck on the table
No voice

Hellooo?

Prizren

This city is proud of its stature and size,

By car it takes an hour,
On foot a hundred years,
You set off counting the trees, the fountains and songs,
The tombstones and eons.
Three generations old when you reach it,
With the weight of time on your back.

Ailing and tired of solitude,
You find an ancient house in town,
Guarded by two ancient men,
One with a necktie and papers,

SABRI HAMITI

A felt cap and pistol, the other.
You measure your age and your loneliness
In the cracked earth, the crumbling roofs,
The smokeless chimneys . . .
And learn of the balance of words and of things.

The fortress above you is silent
With teeth as long as time itself,
Who has known more solitude:
The fortress, the river, or you,
Or Prizren itself, that ancient city?

Ali Podrimja

Let it all be forgotten
Let it all be forgotten

My brother spit in my face
Laughing, guffawing

I saw him weep

Let it all be forgotten

Last night I embraced someone
My friend, forgive me, my friend

I was drunk last night, my friend

Let it all be forgotten.

George Castrioti

Every time the frost comes
We recall Your name,
The first and the second,
We do our best to teach it to the children.

Names arise from the shades of the past.
Nish, Kruja, Albulena, and Berat.
And again the two names: the first and the second,
One for oneself, one for the others.

Every time the frost comes
We recall Your name.
The living, the suffering. What value has life
When nourished by past memories?

The children, who learn names quickly,
Do not want only this, they want more,
They want life, a name for themselves,
The children who do not thrive on memories.

Every time the frost comes
We recall Your name,
When the barking of dogs in the night
Destroys the profound and infinite silence.

A name for oneself and one for the others,
Making amends for life.
Ask the children when they grow up.
They know no memories, only dreams.

SABRI HAMITI

VISAR ZHITI
1952–

Visar Zhiti, born in the port city of Durrës, is the Albanian writer whose life and works perhaps best mirror the history of his nation. He was one of the many to have suffered appalling persecution for no apparent reason. In the wake of a political purge, the manuscript of his first poetry collection was interpreted as containing grave ideological errors and was denounced as anti-Communist agitation and propaganda. At a mock trial, the poet was subsequently sentenced to thirteen years in prison—for poetry, as he tells us—and was exiled to the isolated northern mountains to do the rounds in the infamous concentration camps, similar to the Soviet gulags. Many of his fellow prisoners died of mistreatment and malnutrition, or went mad. Zhiti survived—physically, intellectually, and emotionally—and was released after a seven-year ordeal. He is now among the most popular poets of present-day Albania. His works have appeared in English in the volume *The Condemned Apple: Selected Poetry* (Los Angeles: Green Integer, 2005). Zhiti is also the author of short stories and novels.

At the Bars of My Cell

How sweetly the nightingale sang
Through the iron bars of my window,
Transforming the very iron
    into the verdant branches of a cherry tree.

The floor was covered in warbles,

And I, on my knees,
Picked them up one by one
Like crumbs of bread,
    like crumbs of life.

Little Prison, Big Prison

Do you know the two brothers in prison?

There are also three brothers,
And a father and son.
There are also a grandfather and grandson in prison.
A father-in-law and a son-in-law,
A man and his wife,
(His love languishes in the women's ward
Over hair shorn,
   like a blackbird
With wings clipped that it not soar).

There is also a family in prison,
All together
They've been sentenced to over a century.

Be steadfast!
Our whole country is a prison,
Draped in barbed wire,
Sentenced to three thousand years. Before Christ.
Our little prison
In the belly of a big prison
Is like a baby in the pouch
Of a crazed kangaroo.
You may despair,
But be steadfast!

Death Impresses No One Here

The tunnel caved in
And a prisoner was killed.
(But the chains he was wearing have not yet been killed.)

VISAR ZHITI

And so, the chain gang returned to camp
With one man less,
With one corpse more,
Undelivered to its family for burial.

(You are neither among the living
Nor among the dead.
You have no life,
Not even a grave!)

The jacket worn by the dead prisoner
Is held in the hands of one of his friends.
Throw it at the feet
Of the officer at the gate,
In charge of the watchmen,
And say: "Count it, are we all here?"
Take the jacket
And shield Albania's trembling shoulders.

The Prison Shower Room

We, the prisoners,
Slip out of the black mine
Like twilight shadows from the grave.

We put out our oil lamps,
Throw aside our boots,

And hustle off to the shower room.

Water—the only warmth we have,
Like rain blessed by the heavens,
Pours over our naked bodies.

You wash the exhaustion,
The insults,

The mire of death off your ribs,
Sublime pleasure,
Standing in the steam,
As if in the realm of sleep
You suddenly see yourself
In a dream . . .
You rub your shoulders,
Scrub your arms, belly, and thighs,
Finding nothing foreign on you,
    neither claws,
    nor horns.
The shower weeps a torrent of tears
Over feeble, wounded,
    blackened,
    bodies.
You revel,
Are bewildered,
Could faint for joy,
Fall in love with the water
As it glides over and envelops your body
Like a woman.

And you feel
You have not been abandoned entirely,
Not by the snow which melts
And fills the mighty rivers.

Far from the sea
Are the prisons,
Full of dead waves of life.
Then come the clouds on high,
And then the rain,
Washing the naked nation—a prisoner's body.

The beloved water licks me with its tongue,
Soothing me all over.
The shadow of the barbed wire,
    like a tattoo on a slave,

VISAR ZHITI

Stretches somber on my skin
And I wash and wash,
And fall into another reality,
   Einstein,
   lunar.
Now I can fly
Far, far away. . . .
Vaporized pain.

Bloody Lips

The open wound
Of the gladiator
Gurgles out life's end.

The cries of acclamation from the stands
Fill the sky with raging tigers.

Waving their arms about, to incite the masses,
The aging notables add an air of dignity to the arena.
Making their separate entries, they   k
                                        n
                                        e
                                        e
                                        l over the still-warm corpses
Of the young. Their withered lips they pose
Upon the fresh flowing wounds
And, to prolong their lives—so they believe,
Suck, ravenously suck out the blood, blood, blood.
Fresh blood from the sun,
Flowing into filthy veins
As if into sewage pipes,

And thus the Heart of the Nation is abandoned.

In Our Cells

They keep us in our cells
For a long time . . .

And, if we get out,
We lug them with us on our shoulders,
Like a porter with a chest of goods.

The Tyrant's Onetime Office, Near Which I Work

Cautiously I opened the door of the tyrant's great office,
How odd, I'm filled with fear again, a different kind of fear.
I thought the walls would be spattered
   with the blood of the masses,
That the ashtrays on the long desk would surely be made
Of the skulls of ministers shot dead.
The floorboards did not crackle nervously,
There was no whirlpool of intrigues,
No abyss of convictions. No gun barrels
Emerging from the drawers
   like the eyes of metal detectors.
I stood silent, pallid,
As if just over a long illness.

. . . they were destroying the symbols of tyranny . . .
The noise of the hammers was like
   the dismantling of a guillotine.
Neither occupation, nor earthquakes, nor cholera
Spread by mice in the Middle Ages, nor world wars
Brought this cataclysm upon Albania, but rather
   this much-dreaded office, here!
Before my very eyes hung a crystal chandelier
Like a head chopped off,
   hanging by the hair.

VISAR ZHITI

My Father's Poem

Yellowing pages
From the last world war,
Gnawed on, like desperation.

It is my father's poem, his poor *Iliad*,
Published in many a newspaper at the time
And turned into a play . . . performed
At the Kosova cinema in Tirana . . . Two old people,
They told me, met at that play
And got married (and they're not called Helen
Or Paris). Engaged under the occupation . . .
        But the partisans
Ordered that the poem be burned,
Should it be found. A hostile leaflet. Against the teachings.

While the guards were unloading banned books
And old newspapers from a truck
At the paper factory,
To make new white paper,
        as sterile as oblivion,
A friend of mine who worked there
Plunged his hands into the blades
        of the cutting machine,
Into the mouth of the Minotaur, and surreptitiously
Extracted my father's poem, once banned, the author
And his works. They had sent them to Hades.
Hidden behind walls of fear, we leafed through it:

"Forget not Çameria and hapless Kosova.
They dreamt of freedom, became a dream themselves."

Lines worthy of the nation. Like flies gathering over
The dead body of winter. What are you saying? Save us!

My father
Who art in heaven and under earth . . .

My father died blind, like a begging Homer,
And my mother stopped sewing during the dictatorship.
Me in handcuffs
   they dragged off
   behind a black car
Within the walls of the New Illyria.

Far from Our Countries

Far from our countries, like two Tantaluses
We drank coffee: I and a publisher
   from Belgrade,
We spoke about Kosova in a third language.
It used to be the cradle of Serbia, he said, so we have rights,
But it is full of Albanians, so you have rights.
So, you mean, we should have had more cradles,
   I said. He fell silent.
But let us not turn the cradles into graves, I added sighing,
One's country is an accident, said the publisher from Belgrade.
So let us not lose it accidentally, I added.
We can enrich one another. No one is
   superfluous.

Shall we turn our cups over to read our fate,
My good Serb? Behind yonder mountains in the Balkans
Our future lies waiting. Like the nymphs it rises from the waters
Which flow through the forests and, naked, timidly
Approach the cities. . . .

MARIO BELLIZZI
1957–

Mario Bellizzi, a poet of the Albanian-speaking Arbëresh minority
of southern Italy, was born in San Basile, in the province of Cosenza.

His verse has appeared in various Arbëresh periodicals in southern Italy, as well as in Kosova and Albania. Bellizzi currently lives in Trebisacce, on the Gulf of Taranto. Among his verse collections are *Who Are We Now?* (Peja, 1997) and *Last Exit to Bukura Morea* (Castrovillari, 2003).

Aroma

I hold in my hands
A bouquet of country flowers,
Nakedness incarnadine,
From which course rivers of light,
Silken blossoms with vernal places.
I carry in my palms my fields,
Nakedness incarnadine.

Curfew

Here in Prizren
There is a curfew after one in the morning.
Angels
Dare not dally in the cobblestone lanes,
Or wander down to the Lumbardhi River
To cross the old stone bridge,
And lovers cannot go out hand in hand
To marvel at the mosque and the moon,
At the flags fluttering in the breeze.
Yet from the houses,
Ruined by rockets,
Burst the sounds of the *lahuta,* of drums and shawms!
This will be the hypnotic music
Which fastens the people here
Amidst the tanks and barbed wire,
Immersed in the lure of that Pentagram
Which is the Orient.

Serbs, Coca-Cola, and Kosovars

Mitrovica, Mitro-Vica, Vica-Mitro,
A town divided, bisected.
A neutral zone, that is, a corridor,
Surrounded by barbed wire,
By armed soldiers protected.
In it a drink shop.
One side Serbs, the other Albanians,
And in it Fanta and Coca-Cola.
What madness!

Trance

for my friend, the poet Osman Gashi

The dervishes' power!
In a trance
They can make tanks prance about
In a Prizren ring-around-the-rosy,
Mortars aimed at Kosovar breasts
Can do no harm
If Kosova holds its breath.

ABDULLAH KONUSHEVCI
1958–

Abdullah Konushevci was born and raised in Prishtina, studied literature at the University of Zagreb, and worked for many years as a journalist for the Kosova daily newspaper *Rilindja*. He is noted not only as a leading Kosovar poet but also for his essays and writings on Albanian literature and on the Albanian language.

Konushevci is the author of six volumes of intense verse: *Mirror and Sun* (*Pasqyrë dhe diell* [Prishtina, 1979]), *The Fall of the Apple* (*Rënia e molles* [Prishtina, 1981]), *The Sun's Carriage* (*Qerrja e diellit*

[Prishtina, 1983]), *The Game of the Ostrich* (*Loja e strucit* [Prishtina, 1987]), *The Unbeen Beings* (*Të qenët të mosqenë* [Prishtina, 1990]), and, most recently, *The Drops AD* (*Pikat AD* [Prishtina, 2002]), with its startling reflections on the 1999 war in Kosova. He has also translated, into Albanian, works of Ernest Hemingway, Rabindranath Tagore, and Milovoj Slaviček.

Dream . . . Then Vlora

Once we were on another planet
Where there was bread, milk, and meat,
And none of their militia.

The Albanians were having a grand time,
Lying in the shade,
Prancing in public places,
Making love, great love.

Once . . . then Vlora entered the room:
"Dad, they broke the door down again
At two in the morning,
They, whose name I dare not speak."

Expressionist Verse

The heavens sweat
And reek of blood
From the iron birds
That have rent their breasts.

The masters of death
Are working the land as they know best,
Hurling heads, hands, and feet
Wherever they wish.

How can we sweep up the limbs
Before night falls,
And cremate them in the earth
Before those recluse beasts
Get wind of them?

How Prishtina Once Woke in the Morning

Prishtina once woke to alarm clocks,
And flooded, sleepyheaded, onto the streets,
Damp in the dew,
Aroused from her nightmares.

At noon she gasped for breath,
An asthma patient
Beneath the ashen-gray ballerinas
That danced on her head
The grim steps of death.

In the evening she found no rest
From the barking dogs, the whirring electrons,
And from fear that some unseen beast
Would appear and slit her throat.

The Honorable Whore

I met her after I know not how many glasses
That night,
The blood had not yet dried on the streets,
People still smelled
The heavy earth of graves in their nostrils. . . .

ABDULLAH KONUSHEVCI

I remember she was of lissome body
And had blue, such blue eyes. . . .
I know I offered her a glass of brandy
And she offered me another. . . .

When we woke the next morning
We separated as friends.
I remember we had drunk brandy together
As comrades in adversity.

Heavy Burden, Your Fragile Body

With my gnawed liver,
With my lashed lungs,
With my fingers stained and tarred from nicotine,
I am of no use to anyone.

I cannot believe
That you would be foolish enough
To bestow your love on me.

I don't know what to do
With my insomnia,
With those shadows of fallen friends.

Heavy burden,
Your fragile body.

BESNIK MUSTAFAJ
1958–

Besnik Mustafaj was born in Bajram Curri, in the Tropoja region of
the northern Albanian mountains. He studied French at the Univer-

sity of Tirana and, after the collapse of the Communist dictatorship, was seconded as Albanian ambassador to France. Active not only as a writer but also in political life, he was appointed foreign minister of the Republic of Albania in the autumn of 2005.

Mustafaj is both a prose writer and poet. His poetry has appeared in the collections *Merry Motifs* (*Motive të gëzuara* [Tirana, 1978]), *Face of a Man* (*Fytyrë burri* [Tirana, 1987]), and *The Legend of My Birth* (*Legjenda e lindjes sime* [Tirana, 2005]). His prose works, including novels and essays, have been translated into French, German, and Bulgarian.

The Heroes and I

The heroes were huge when I was little,
Larger than the figures of their statues.
As I grew
I looked at them
Less and less
From below
Until one day we were eye to eye.

What will happen now?
Will I, or will the heroes, learn
Which of us is superfluous?

Donika

We speak of George,
    of his long days and nights at war,
Of the savage sieges, victories,
Of his clever courser, his strong sword,
But we often forget you.

We forget how he returned battle-weary
To find you waiting at the door.
Your body took on his anguish at the wounds of his fallen soldiers,
At seeing fields of grain torched,
    At glimpsing wells drained of their water,
So that he would have nothing.

He had to rest a while
To be ready for combat the next day.
His head, which never bowed to heavy cannons,
Yielded to your soft shoulder.

You watched as his lids grew heavy,
As his eyes closed,
And, to make his dreams sweeter,
You entered them yourself.

If you were needed in those long sieges,
You are needed all the more in eternity.
How could we otherwise claim to know
    the true George,
Without that part of him he left with you?

Night Walk in the Forest

The trees, the stones, the grass, the flowers are mute.
And I, belated wanderer, sing so as
Not to let them languish in the nocturnal silence.

I am alone in that silence,
But when I sing, night is no longer night,
And I am no longer alone,
I hear the footsteps of my beloved,
And the birds beat their wings,

The trees rustle their branches,
Over my blue shirt
The crickets awaken the summer sun,
I see how my beloved closes her eyes
To cling to me there for a moment,
I become air, water, light, and fire on her lips.

The forest, which can no longer keep still,
Falls back and stops somewhere behind me,
So as not to interrupt my song. . . .

Prophetic Poem

If, instead of Christ and Muhammad,
The Bible and the Koran
Had written of the tragic fate
   of Tristan and Isolde,
Exemplary lovers,
Mortals on this tiny planet,
They would have had a hard time denying
The concept of the divine.

I've Set Off to Find You

There you are,
So close and yet unreachable,
Like the Moon.

I've set off like a crusader to find you.
Can't you see what a state I'm in?
By one hand Dante's hauling me toward Hell,
By the other, Don Quixote's pulling me toward . . .

And I don't know where you are.
Are you Beatrice or Dulcinea?

And yet . . .

Whence Your Fear of the Wolf

My son, you were born in the city
And have never set foot
    in the dark forest.
Where did you get that terrible fear
    of the wolf?

What is a wolf, I ask you,
What is it like, I inquire.

You only know it's rapacious
And when it's hungry,
Waters bloodied by lambs
    are churned up to their very source,
Stopping the flocks from quenching their peaceful thirst.

Yet I tell you, you've never seen a wolf,
    my little one.
How odd, in this big city.
Whence your fear of the wolf?

BASRI ÇAPRIQI
1960–

Basri Çapriqi is a leading poet of the Albanian community in Montenegro. He was born in Krytha, near Ulqin (Ulcinj), on the Adriatic coast. Çapriqi studied Albanian language and literature at the

University of Prishtina, from which he received his doctorate in 2004. He teaches stylistics and semiology at that university and is currently head of the Kosova PEN Centre.

Çapriqi is the author of six volumes of verse, the most recent of which is *Weird Fruits* (*Frutat bizare* [Prishtina, 1996]). He has also published literary studies and anthologies.

My Room in London

the traditional english-style window and the mirrors around it in-crease the illusion of space you watch me from the street and from the surrounding apartments i cannot lock anything with the key that binds me to you the thames takes it all and casts it down by the two flanks of my naked body surrounded by mirrors that increase the illusion of infinite space in my bedroom i cannot lock this cubic world with the key that separates me from you the thames takes my little belongings and i cannot find them in the shadows suffocating me as they parade in the mirrors that extend the size of my bedroom the traditional english-style window and the confusing key in the open door fracture the light into a multitude of views of my limbs hanging in the mirrors that turn to ruins my world hidden from public view and the masses.

My Room in Ulqin

Even when I am not there
My mother opens the shutters to the sea.

The moon floods in, outlined in a glass,
Filling the room with my figure.

My mother flings the shutters open to the sea
Even when I am not there

To bring in the fresh salt air,
For I am breathing somewhere
On the crest of a breeze
When she leaves the door open.

Girl from the East, Prostitute in Rome

They pay good money here
Full stop
In Prague the minister of food production arraigned me
In the name of the people
Full stop

I was a member of the Party

They pay good money here full stop
And the minister of heavy industry
And the people
Full stop

And I'm not permitted to be a member of their
Party

That is the main difference
Full stop
Buona notte.

MIMOZA AHMETI
1963–

Mimoza Ahmeti, from Kruja, is one of the *enfants terribles* of the
nineties, who set about to expand the horizons and explore the pos-
sibilities offered to her by her own senses. Dragging the nation, in
her idiosyncratic manner, along the bumpy road to Europe, she has

managed in recent years to provoke Albania's impoverished and weary society into much-needed reflection that, with time, may lead to new and more sincerely human values. After two volumes of verse in the late eighties, it was the fifty-three poems in the collection *Delirium* (Tirana, 1994) that caught the public's attention. Ahmeti's poetry has been well received by the new generation of readers in tune, for the first time, with Western culture. Her candid expressions of wide-eyed feminine desire and indulgence in sensual pleasures and the crystalline fluidity of her language have already made of her a modern classic. The traditional polarization of male and female verse seems to have dissolved under the passionate force of her quill.

Mental Asylum with Open Doors

You are going, you are leaving us,
Thinking it's *forever.*
Fleeing from this, which is yours, ours,
Which is our mental asylum,
Our beloved, moving asylum
With skulls dismembered.

O my sacred madmen,
How I love you,
Though I never speak to you,
Though you never speak to me
And I cannot stand you
And you cannot stand me.
But such are the rites:
We never look each other in the eye
Without hating one another,
And such is the motive
For loving one another mad,
While smiling in exaltation,
And all the while
Tears flow down our cheeks,
Tears.

MIMOZA AHMETI

Fellow sufferers
Of our unique madness,
You who are setting off into exile,
With eyes fixed
On one sole idea,
Yes, only one sole idea,
Which has never been seen, never been found,
And I doubt if it ever will be found.

Be off, depart, disappear.
From place to place, from country to country . . .
Oh, what shrieking echoes
From our asylum
As the sun sets late in the west,
When longing lingers for its children in the West . . .

What sorrow!
Bare walls . . . Walls which always
   block the horizon
And leave an infinite sky above.

There, after midnight, the sobbing subsides,
Someone is talking to himself:
Nonetheless, the Albanians,
Wherever they may be,
Make do with their own madness. . . .

Delirium

Broken,
   somber,
   venomous
I stand, light-emitting,
Honey flows from my fissures,
Shattered at my weakest point,

Alone and abandoned,
A state that causes harm to no one,
But me it destroys
In pain
Which drips with the sweet aroma
Of blood crushed
In solitude.

Oh, ingenious is this state,
For as I come to understand that I have lost everything,
I sense the infinite pleasure
Of having in hand
My own being,
Which
Neither praise nor crown
Could ever have bestowed on me.

Praise! What word is this?
How did it reach me?
How did it come?
An invention!
(Certainly
Some base, unnatural
Ambition.)

I return whence I came, and arrive at nature.
Here I stand, want to judge it, but once again withdraw.
How fair and yet mortal is man,
How hearty and yet lonely.
Such strength and such suspicion . . .

Oh, unceasingly
You survey that inert unwinding in flight.
Everything absolute becomes unexpected.
Has only beauty the right
To pretend?

MIMOZA AHMETI

Why do you shun me, real creatures?
In a fugitive transformation, my today
Became my yesterday,
So swiftly that it was beyond my comprehension
(Do you think there is life without that?)
Desire is yearning for a tomorrow
Which is not mine.

Why do you shun me, real creatures?
I live a life of objects forever inexistent
And have only myself in my hands. . . .
Oh, is there any greater bliss than this?
Could there be any greater sorrow?

Eastern Europe

O race of the steers of passion
Which gives life to my veins,
O tranquillity of oppression, stoic observation, the pulsing
Steam . . .
I feel no pity and forgive no one,
Take account of nothing.
Go ahead and explode,
Depart. . . .

O purity of the East, fresh budding fears
Of muscles and the blood of origin.
Brain ringing, temples resounding,
Echoing within the skull, silence outside.
Outside, dust.
Only dust that sings
   and rules the world.
Raises and fells the musty forms
Of human effigies:
Some gestures, sounds, impulses—
Extinction once again.

O fresh fears budding like steers
In my veins,
How can I control you, set you free, clash blood-smeared
   with you?
Or let you freely exit the arena
With my blood which you have inseminated?

O crucified cries in the empty recesses of my mind,
O knives of pain which shatter on my skull,
O pride, strength, attribution of the explosion.
Insanity—clear conscience.

Death

O eternal and omnipotent silence,
From you I arose, in an endeavor
To return to you.
But, more arduous is the going back. . . .
I was a child at the time,
Now I am grown.

I'm Just Mad About Campari

I love Campari sooooooo much.
My wife, no, she doesn't drink it.
I talk to her for five minutes a week
And I'm not number one in her books.
Oh, I'm just mad about Campari. . . .

But I don't plan to die
   this way.
No, I am not gonna die like this.
I'm going back to America to face up to things
Then I'll come back here.

MIMOZA AHMETI

249

But, did you know that Campari can be drunk
Refined with soda water and lemon?
It's sooooooo sooooooo delicious.
Campari. I just love it.
America is one huge supermarket. . . .
That's where I lost my way
And found it, you know where?
In the Campari.
Hemingway loved it,
Not women . . .
Hemingway . . . wasn't the first
To love Campari. . . .

Do you wanna come to America with me?
What? "To lose your way?"
Wonderful. Is that what they call "irony"?

I'm just mad about Campari. . . .
She is the girl
I'm in love with.

Letter to Mommy

Mommy,
Don't let anyone but you read this letter,
Not because it's secret, I'm just not strong enough yet
To deal with what I'm telling you.
Tirana is its same old self,
The narrow alleys and low houses,
The weary wintry roads,
A fifteen-story building in the middle,
Built like my utopia,
Watchmen on street corners near the embassies,
Police—woodpeckers of a waning June.

I sense that something is about to happen, Mommy,
The government was never so much against the people,
Never was treachery among men so much in fashion,
Never did more lost and more empty women
Drift through the nights in such a deep sleep.

I tell you, Mommy, peril is summoning me
With the toothless smile of a hungry love,
With a rift in its character,
Part of the rift in society,
They are offering me jobs, many of my friends and acquaintances,
All with high names in society, but low in life's tension,
Helping me to climb the ladder by using me,
But causing my fall, not raising me at all.

Dear mother, listen to me, don't worry,
With my verses,
I will chop them up, grind them to bits, I tell you,
Like a mincing machine.

FLUTURA AÇKA
1966–

Flutura Açka was born in Elbasan, in central Albania, and gradu-
ated in economics in 1988 from the University of Tirana. She worked
for a number of years as a journalist in Elbasan and for the Onufri
publishing company before founding her own publishing company,
Skanderbeg Books.

As a poet, Açka first gained wide recognition when she received
the Lyre of Struga award at the 1997 International Nights of Poetry
festival held in Struga, Macedonia. Among her major publications
are the poetry volumes *Three Autumns Away* (*Tri vjeshta larg* [El-
basan, 1993]), *Walls of Solitude* (*Mure vetmie* [Elbasan, 1995]), *Feast
with Anguish* (*Festë me ankthin* [Elbasan, 1997]), *The Song of Arethusa*
(*Kënga e Aretuzës* [Prishtina, 1998]), *The Sun Trap* (*Kurth' i diellit*
[Tirana, 2003]), and the short novel *A Woman's Solitude* (*Vetmi gru-*

aje [Tirana, 2001]). A volume of her poetry has been translated into Macedonian.

Landscape

The mountains are clad in white-flannel breeches,
Black-braided seams, torrents tumble and vanish in the vales,
Haze here and there still hovers o'er hillsides,
Tufts of billowing wool.

The wind for a moment forgot its roar and rumble,
Snowy silence, boundless and virgin, clad
In the white splendor of long months of bridehood,
Mountain passes still retain their winter borage.

From afar they are bride and pensive bridegroom,
Gathered at noble wedding.
Toward them I pace, forgetting
Rice to throw over their ridges.

On Our "Ancestral Lands"

From that moment on,
I left behind me the void of my steps,
The traces of my unlived life.
Where did all the words go?
Where did we vanish
Who are no longer?

Thereafter,
White wastelands of repentance,
Topographies of torment,
Neither you
Nor I

Know
Whence the storm has come.

From that moment on,
They became my scarf of oblivion
To wrap and warm the late nights, and yet,
How cold it is on our "ancestral lands"!

Prayer for Anna Akhmatova

How it now spins, how it hovers between us,
That invention called love, as the poet once said,
When you put it out, you put me on fire,
Silently glowing in ashes of dread.

Why does it wait for the cold winds of winter?
Why does it hold back the torrents in May?
Like a devilish child that has now been awakened,
A new dream is born and will soon go its way.

Let sleep take care of your fears and your anguish,
Let nighttime abscond now with your every tear,
And when you awake somewhere up in the heavens
An eclipse of the heart will have taken place here.

Monotony

In that same street,
With those same steps,
Under those same trees
We meet,
With the very same expressions
On that most monotonous and
Most genuine of mornings.

Gray hair,
The only change
In the heavy air of time.

Ballad on a Campaign to Inhibit Feelings

That eyes not fail us
We invented glasses.

That hands not quiver
We invented pockets.

What help can we find
For our hearts?

Evil Doings

I left behind a part of my soul
When I was born
As a hostage
For this world's evil doings.

And when I die, the evildoers
Will certainly say:
"It was your doing!"

ARIAN LEKA
1966–

Arian Leka is a leading contemporary writer from the port city of
Durrës. He is editor in chief of the well-received poetry periodical

Poeteka: Review of Poetry and Poetic Culture (Poeteka: Revistë e Poezisë dhe e Kulturës Poetike).

Among Leka's publications are the short story collections *This Quiet Country Where Nothing Ever Happens* (*Ky vend i qetë ku s'ndodh asgjë* [Tirana, 1994]) and *The Sins of the Dead* (*Veset e të vdekurve* [Tirana, 1997]), the novel *The House Snake* (*Gjarpri i shtëpisë* [Tirana, 2002]), and the verse collections *The Ship of Sleep* (*Anija e gjumit* [Tirana, 2000]) and *Strabismus* (*Strabizëm* [Tirana, 2004]).

The Spine of the Sea

My people turned their spines to the sea.

And I have the same inclination,
I sink ships,
Drill holes in their hulls
And flee afar
To where clouds are the fish,
Where every grave is a barge with a white sail,
Where every tree bears fruit in its belly,
And the ships . . .
The ships depart
Because my people turned their spines to the sea
And netted naught
But the sweet food of the land
And its drink.

Alone

Profound is solitude in two glasses of wine,
A ruddy horse and a white horse.
Nothing is as it seems to be
When you have it all and no one to share it.

ARIAN LEKA

Soon it will rain and the doors will be shut,
Those inside are in, no others will make it,
Two glasses of wine, a black horse in the jug,
I now have it all, but no one to share it.

Easter on the Island of Hvar

The sea eats stone eggs
And breaks its teeth on the banks:
Salty islands, poison cactus,
Rosemary and the oil of lamps
That departed to return no more,
Brides kidnapped by the wind,
Maidens bitten by pirates.

My soul walks over these waters
That saw me in an Easter dream.
Six bell towers—hallelujah!
The sea breaks stone eggs—ouch!
I break a milk tooth
On a glass of dry wine.

Six o'clock. Humanity at church.
The sea with me outside.

Background Chant

How can you sing over a grave,
O cuckoo,
Where the earth thrusts cypress trees
Like knives into its sides and flanks,
Where the sky dies insane
Of an overdose of solitude?

Could you not,
Could you not,
Little bird,
Have revived with your song
One single man?

AGRON TUFA
1967–

Agron Tufa was born in Suhadoll, in the Dibra region of eastern Albania, and studied literature at the University of Tirana. He continued his studies in Moscow in the 1990s, where he graduated in translation theory from the Gorky Institute of Literature, with a particular concentration on the work of Joseph Brodsky. Since his return to Albania, he has been involved in the literary magazine *Suitable* (*E për-7-shme*) and edited the much-admired periodical *Aleph*. He is now editor of the literary supplement *The Word* (*FjalA*) and teaches literature at the University of Tirana.

Tufa has published poetry and prose of note. He is the author of the verse collections *There at the Scaean Gates* (*Aty te portat Skée* [Elbasan, 1996]) and *The Surrounding of Atlantis* (*Rrethinat e Atlantidës* [Tirana, 2002]) and the well-received novels *The Duel* (*Dueli* [Tirana, 2002]) and *Fabula Rasa* (*Fabula rasa* [Tirana, 2002]). He has also translated many Russian authors, including Joseph Brodsky, Anna Akhmatova, Osip Mandelstam, Boris Pasternak, Andrei Platonov, Mikhail Bulgakov, Vladimir Nabokov, and Vladimir Sorokin.

Old Stanza for a New Love

for Elvana

When we, without a word, lie down for the night
You will be the River, I will be the Log
And hardly will you be able, with your lips pressed on mine,

In squirming and quivers, to detach from my body. . . .
Nowhere will you spill a crumb,
And I will envy neither the living nor the dead.

Then, they will baptize us . . . Yet you, unwearied
In the flow . . . You will be the River which bears the Log,
One day promised to five oceans.
I will be a banner for those tribes.
And if we find no fair names
I will perhaps call you Anna.

As if borrowed, the years which never return
From winter to winter will tumble to their fate.
Light and long the road we embark on,
Like every vehicle which strays from its goal,
The frontiers will appear in the end,
Though we have journeyed but half the way.

I will be naked, you will be bare,
The two of us crossing hills and vales.
In the law of the flow we will willingly leave
That land, where we never had foes,
And mighty hands on other banks
Will one day meet in that dry bed.

Albania

Albania is greater than its soil,
Than the sky stretching upward above it.
It is the ancient dream of a ship,
A yacht kissing the depths.

It flaps and flutters in two halves,
Wings beating to sear bloody wounds.
It is not part of this planet, but a star,
A tear fallen from the eye of the Lord.

The Regulations at the Catholic School for Girls

The fine fragrance of writing hovered in their midst:
One could hear the arid crackle of mice munching biscuits,
Yet, it was a weary winter
That found them unprepared,
My majestic lovers.
All day long they aged in the classroom,
Salting their tender bowels
With talk of love. Vanished and
Forgotten was that distant day in April . . .
My chance appearance in the library
Came, it seemed, to a sad conclusion.
And in the end, the snow blasted and blew in all directions,
Every day a new storm.
They woke and rose, those wretched maidens,
With time unmoved in their beds.
I spread word of a distant age,
But where,
Where was I at that moment of crisis
When the dreams of my lovers
Turned tiresome and troubled?
Misfortune pelted like a hailstorm,
They found me nailed to my bed
In the most obscure of military hospitals in that town.
Now it was too late,
With poisoned milk in their breasts
They told me their tales in haste
. . . .
And they cursed any future joy I might have,
Making tiny crosses on the cards
With their faded fingers. According
To my lovers (though pale their faces)
I would never be able to leave the hospital,
And yet, I did,
And found them blithe and all with child.
I saw their bellies like fresh tombs
From which wafted a fine fragrance of writing

AGRON TUFA

And rustled to no avail
The licit sound of mice
Still reveling
With dry biscuits in the grass.

The Proof of the Land

The year had twelve seasons all summer long.
Fowl fled . . .
The lone, elegiac poplar
Signed a contract with the grass.
Entered a man with a hatchet
And sampled some of the pale poplar's pith,
Yet, it depends on how he filched it.
At any rate, with some pain in the flesh.
But the man is no longer,
Nor the grass,
Nor the poplar.
In all this struggle of annihilation
The grass wins out over the tomb.
The dead man now comprehends
That it isn't a question of pride, but of life.
Yet, he sighs for posterity.
How many seasons will the springtime have?
God only knows what will happen with the light. . . .
God only knows what will happen with God. . . .
And the lord continues his undoing.

The rains fall stagnant, salacious,
To affirm in grandeur their denial.

Ponderous, the proof of the land.

LULJETA LLESHANAKU
1968–

Luljeta Lleshanaku was born in Elbasan, in central Albania, and is the author of four poetry collections. She studied literature at the University of Tirana and was editor in chief of the weekly magazine *The Voice of Youth* (*Zëri i Rinisë*). She later worked for the literary newspaper *Drita* (*The Light*). In 1996, she received the best book of the year award from the Eurorilindja Publishing House. In 1999, she took part in the International Writing Program at the University of Iowa. A volume of her verse has appeared in English, translated by Henry Israeli et al., under the title *Fresco* (New York: New Directions, 2002).

With You

I will sit in an alcove of your mouth
As on a stone near a waterfall
Certain that the maelstrom of words will not spirit me away.

I will crouch in the corner of your eye
Like a lily sprouting in the shallows near the shore
With petals tiny so as not to distract.

For after all, what am I?
A frozen wave in space
Wrested from the sea of your chest,
You stretch your hands toward me in vain.

Annual Snowfall

In this town
The annual snowfall
Hanging on the rare and solitary trees

Brings nothing new.
It is merely
A veteran out on his daily stroll
Leaning on his wooden cane.

The same tales of war
Told a hundred times,
The same brand of cigarettes offered in friendship
And the same eyes accompany him
Dark and lazy,
And the dry rhythmic tap of his cane
Until his silhouette disappears
Into the long shadows of rooftops
Dripping
In terrible slowness. . . .

Mutual Understanding

    for my two-year-old daughter Lea

I cannot escape your sunflower gaze,
Do not judge me for what I lack,
A maternal instinct
Which like a water bottle grown cold
Ends up at the foot of the bed.

Understand me, I am like you,
Ever curious about what goes on between two people,
Just like you
I suspect it is something without a history,
Like an apple you bite into only once
And then cast away with no remorse.

Chamomile Breath

We never spoke a word about death, Mother,
Just as married couples never talk about sex,
Just as doctors never use the word "blood,"
Just as the mailman never needs to say "news,"
And frogmen never need to mention "air."

Yet fear adorns everything you touch,
The same way the gait of black harvesters
Causes the cotton fields to quiver.

In the morning
Your chamomile breath
Escapes like a lamb
From the sheep pen.
On the wrinkled pillow
Are unfamiliar white hairs,
And metallic black hair clips.

Do not expect it to arrive loudly
In motley dress
With bells attached to its elbows and knees
Like carnival clowns
Or morris dancers at the end of May.

You will never see the carnival clowns!

You will see a child with spindly legs and a thick crop of hair
Who had no time to grow up.
Did you never hear them say
That death is as close to birth
As two nostrils to one another
Letting out a deep groan?

Always a Premonition

A premonition? . . . Or is it the stench of alcohol
On the mailman's breath as he brings me a tardy
Letter?
A foreshadowing
Always appears before me
Like a long-thighed ostrich
In blithe departure.

Wherever it goes
It marks my tardy will,
There will always be a sign, some thick and greasy
Feather
Of its white prepotency.

By accident you wipe my kisses off your face
With the rest of the shaving cream clinging to your ears.
An intuition . . . another warning and
I ought to be careful . . . The termites are restless
When they fear to go out in the damp soil . . . Always a
       premonition . . .
I return exhausted to my daily routine
Like a vacuum cleaner sucking up yesterday's dust
And all sorts of other unpredictabilities
With a black cord wound around my feet.

The Old People's Home

A rusty-colored gate, no name,
The passage to the old people's home.

Amidst the stones in the yard
The grass has withered
Under the weight of many canes.

Behind the curtains, on the windowsills
Dentures float
In water glasses here and there,
Like messages in bottles bobbing on the high sea
Never to be read.

The gate to the old people's home,
Bearing two sad numbers,
Is always opened in silence
And hesitation,
Like the Bible's much-thumbed pages.

Quite by Accident

And yet
I recognized
That beloved face
Lacerated by the green grille.
I felt it
And, taking a deep breath in the desert wind,
I smelled
That face,
With someone else's hand on my back.
The wheels of time broke loose
And my breast whined like a well,
Like the metallic splash of an empty bucket
Plunging swiftly to the bottom.

But now I know we are strangers
And are here beside each other quite by accident,
Like the photos of two victims
(from the crash of a large airplane)
On the front page of the daily news.

Electrolysis

Your kisses have long been singeing me like a wound
And your pristine body
Frightens me
Like the sheets in the surgery ward,
And your breath fades in a corner of my lungs
Like a forgotten lily on a wintry park bench.

They have long been ashamed of my freedom
Which every day yanks a stake off your fence
In the fire of which
I warm my shanks, blue with cold from flight.

My freedom . . . your freedom . . . our common freedom,
Defined once and forever, sealed within a jar.
An atmosphere of electrolysis. A muffled sound,
My soul being nickeled and yours waning thinner every day,
Deserted by the ions.

For as Long As

For as long as we mirror one another
Like this, even distorted
In silver spoons, on glasses and on bubbly bottles
On the board of a dinner party about to begin,
Things cannot be going that badly.
Soon the soulless steam of hot food will hiss in,
And then . . .
The flood of death will be at hand.

The Truth

The truth is someone else's privilege, when a soul
Approaches, lock your door, let it pass
As the Jews did, forewarned in Egypt,
When it accosts your lips, show no mercy,
Chew it up like a piece of liver
And force it back to its warm embitterment.
If you spit it out
I will be the first to haunt you,
My prayers will isolate you more and more every day,
They will expose your broad shoulders,
Undefended cathedrals.

So recently banished, we are always too late
To stop and ask why we are here,
Why we were born wearing but a single leaf,
The sallow swipe of a purulent potter.

We search for a clean body to lean on,
All this would be a tale of thorns
Saturated in the sunlight.
Let me touch, there is only one truth,
The one which hands gently stroke,
The others are white clouds lurking
As ever in a Turkish steam bath.

The truth is someone else's privilege. Did you not notice?
We would never have withstood
The solitude of the water
Like two weathered stone angels
On the rim of a fountain.

LINDITA ARAPI
1972–

Lindita Arapi was born in Lushnja, between Tirana and Vlora. Following her studies at the University of Tirana, she began working as a journalist and moderator for Albanian television (TVSH). She was awarded a fellowship as a writer in residence at the Heinrich Böll House (Düren, Germany) in 1996 and a scholarship by the International Art Link (New York). She has also taken part in the International Writing Program of the University of Iowa as an honorary fellow in writing. She received her doctorate from the University of Vienna and currently lives in Bonn.

Arapi, who is among the leading female poets of the post-Communist generation from Albania, has published three volumes of verse: *Corpse of Flowers* (*Kufomë lulesh* [Tirana, 1993], translated into Italian as *Il cadavere fiorito* [Brindisi, 1993]), *It Happened in My Soul* (*Ndodhi në shpirt* [Elbasan, 1995]), and *Melody of Silence* (*Melodi të heshtjes* [Peja, 1998]).

Walls

And if a wall, long and thick,
A high wall
Should rise in front of you . . .
What would you do?

I would close my eyes, I would crouch
And rest my cheek against it,
I would find peace in its cool serenity.

And if this wall were death . . .

Energies of Color

O innocence, disrobed yet white,
And you
Sincerity, scarlet yet sinful,
Is there any shadow in your colors
Where you can take refuge and rest your thoughts for a moment?
Has this foolhardiness
Any meaning at all,
Or will it come to rest like silk when the wind dies down,
Seductive silk settling soft and slow?
I am afraid, afraid for you,
O white.

White is murderous.
It will cut down your cleanliness,
Oozing
Little drops of blood
From severed fingers,
Breathless, but with ambiance.

Red,
Red is a cold color,
Lost energy,
Stunning dissonance,
It is a color which offers everything . . . while in your hand.
So naive,
Though it gives nothing
Without fear of black,
Burns you in scarlet reflection,
And comes to rest only when rain recovers it
Unquenched without water.

O innocence, disrobed yet white,
And you
Sincerity, scarlet yet sinful,
Insensitive, you stand to one side,

Punished and obedient,
You raise the intensity of color.
A line of perfection with crippling barriers.

Bloodstain

To recline
In a room of *white*
On cushions of *white*
They enter,
The natives in their skullcaps of *white*,
And sit,
Wiping their brows with kerchiefs of *white*,
And drink
Coffee from scalding cups of *white*,
They greet
The bride all dressed in *white*
And wish her offspring
On frosty days of *white*,
Then to the feast
They rise
And slay sheep of *white*.

Girls Are Made of Water

Girls have only
Moonlit paths
Where they tread like the strains of a violin
Toward the forbidden fruit
    urged on by the wind,
    the clement, warm wind
    which brings the rain,
To and fro in their white and slender veils

They swing and sway to the azure heavens.
And onward they tread
Like the strains of a violin.

Girls have wondrous worlds
    in their watery imagination.
They perish in your hands.
They never find the only way
There is to dream.
No one feeds them.
They hurry forth,
Growing up so terribly fast.
Disrobing in rundown lodgings
They sacrifice themselves,
For girls perish
As soon as they are grown. . . .
Despite their earthly
Urges
They remain UNATTAINABLE
For
They live no longer than a sigh.

PARID TEFERIÇI
1972–

Poet and painter Parid Teferiçi was born and raised in Kavaja, south
of the port of Durrës. From 1990 to 1994, he studied computer
science at the University of Tirana, and from 1994 to 1999, he stud-
ied economics at Bocconi University in Milan. From 1999 to 2001,
he served as head archivist at the library of the Don Calabria In-
stitute in Rome, and in 2001 he became curator of the visual arts
section of the Cini Cultural Institute in Ferrara. He has exhibited
his paintings in Italy. In 2005, he returned to Albania to take part in
the parliamentary elections as a candidate for the Republican Party
in his native Kavaja.

Teferiçi has published two slender volumes of poetry: *Made from a Distance* (*Bërë me largësi* [Tirana, 1996]) and *Since the Eyes* (*Meqenëse sytë* [Tirana, 2003]). His discriminating works have proven him to be among Albania's major contemporary poets.

In Obot, While Waiting

In Obot, as he waited for the ferry to take them over to Bar, Gjergj Nikolla decided to while away the time by cheering up his twelve-year-old son (it was the first time the lad had been away from Shkodra). He took a stone, flung it across the Buna, and invited him to outdo him if he could. The son smiled at the unexpected challenge from his father, chose a stone with great care, and clambered down to the riverside.

Clasping the stone to throw it farther than his father's and perhaps even to the other bank, he felt a sharp pain in the palm of his hand. His wish was simply to hurl the stone and the pain as far away as he could. But he did not outdo his father, and he still has the pain to this day.

In Perspective

... sarebbe stato il più leggiadro e capriccioso ingegno
che avesse avuto da Giotto in qua l'arte della pittura,
se egli si fusse affaticato tanto nelle figure ed animali,
quanto egli si affaticò e perse tempo nelle cose di prospettiva.

Vasari

DONATELLO
Carts in perspective roll on one wheel;
Horses hide behind their tails; trees—beneath the grass,
And people have no hands to greet one another.
What remains of us beyond our visual perception?

PAOLO UCCELLO

Man, in perspective, *is* his visual perception.
Our strongest point, our ultimate strength,
Is the fact that we appear when seen from a distance.
Levers of light, with it and only with it,
Succeed in exalting us to our dignity.

DONATELLO

Distance is the wall which separates us
From the truth, from forms.

PAOLO

It is the wall where truth casts its shadow
And we can draw forms.

DONATELLO

But there, the light, though bright, is not enough.
How can our visual perception ever suffice?

PAOLO

Do not confuse visual perception with light,
As death confuses the farmer with his fields.

DONATELLO

Exactly, in perspective, we are dead.

PAOLO

We are our visual perception. Death—a form.

Woman Holding a Balance, by Vermeer

She is pregnant, and impatience is silently ruminating on her lust for
unseasonable fruit (the spherical impatience of light).

The equanimity of the weighing! The squirming concentration!
Seasick from such a balancing act!

PARID TEFERIÇI

273
.

From the left, light floods in over a jeweled scale. On the side of the weights, one might have added a portion from the painting *The Last Judgment*. But it hangs, hovering on the waxen wall—the condemned, the saved, Christ in a swollen gland, all of them preoccupied with Righteousness.

Then suddenly, serenity—a shaft parallel to the table, to the frame of the *Judgment*.

Yet, the pensive smile of the lady is veiled in oblique rays,

Of the lady who cherishes deep within her the bubble of the spirit level.

The Poet

They shoot at me where I am not to be found.

It comes to pass that they raise my hand from the table
To see if I am not hiding there.
It comes to pass that I must give way
To someone hastening by in search of me.
It comes to pass that they set me on fire
To look for me in the darkness.

However much I stand with my back against the wall
They do not shoot me.

First Prayer

The virgin R hesitates to undo the first button

Can a blossom veil its own fragrance?
How can a zebra hide in one black stripe,
Or a cat in a *fa diesis* meow?
Or an epic journey
In some cheap souvenir?
Can time take refuge
In a suitcase, big though it may be?
How, indeed, could a day,
On a strict schedule,
Conceal itself in a closet
And play hide-and-seek with life?

Can the heavens hide in a breath of air,
Wounds in scabs, the sea in a wave?
Could one of us ever
Hide in the two of us?
How, then, can you hide
In my love for you?

In a Country as Small as This One

The Albanian Leviathan is a sardine. The sitting rooms where men
gather are tins of sardines. Truth, in order to find space there, has
to be folded in two and then folded again.

In a country as small as this, so small that you could easily draw it on
a one-to-one scale on this packet of cigarettes, you don't know where
and how to sit or support yourself: on the throat of your neighbor, or
on the buttocks of the other fellow's wife.
Seated, huddled around the coffee table, how can you greet anyone
without jabbing someone else with your elbow? How can you pay a
compliment without deafening someone?
We can see one another in our spoons, and we are warped.

PARID TEFERIÇI

ROMEO ÇOLLAKU
1973–

Romeo Çollaku was born in the southern port town of Saranda, across from the island of Corfu in neighboring Greece. He studied Albanian language and literature at the University of Gjirokastra and now lives in Athens. Çollaku, a writer of Albanian verse of high linguistic finesse, has published three collections of poems: *Virgin Heart* (*Zemër virgjine* [Tirana, 1993]), *All Sun and Night* (*Gjithë diell e natë* [Tirana, 2003]), and *The Piggy Bank of Time* (*Kumbaraja e kohës* [Tirana, 2004]). He has also published a novel, *Hometown Cemetery* (*Varrezat e vendlindjes* [Tirana, 2002]), and Albanian translations of the poets Yannis Ritsos, Jorgos Seferis, Paul Verlaine, and Stéphane Mallarmé.

The Piggy Bank of Time

As twilight descends, casting black ink upon the village, and the dog's eyes in the courtyard are like two spent oil lamps, you at the windowsill show not your elbows, nor do you bestow a glance on the plum trees or on the fences in the lane.

"On the Night of Saint Demetrius, there is time enough for sleep and thought," chides one of those voices which hardly whispers, and you sit there dazed for hours on end.

And, when you finally get up, you accidentally shatter a porcelain vase (a custom of old, and there is nothing you can do).

Light the lamp and study the gray coins of your childhood scattered upon the floor.

Lost in Thought

Mist and naked plum trees and a madrigal of rain from the rooftop.

There, where the old women tell children tales and croon ballads with magic numbers, stretching to their mouths spoonfuls of bogeymen and sweets: Come on, or the Iron-Toothed One will get you! The jackals once loped through the snow and surrounded the village! An angry ogre had seized the spring.

Three mountains, seven heads, nine cradles . . .
And the obedient children ate, slowly munching and staring, obsessed, at the glimmer beyond the window.

Song of the Horned Lark

Its song was indeed an opaque mutter; feather-light body, freed of life's heavy burden.

For wherever it went, untold weariness, sorrow, and despair.

Now a black spot on the fields grows ever smaller,

Just as, midst snowdrifts at night, the parson's silhouette hastens to church from the house of some wavering soul.

Old Faded Photographs

Brittle, as if no tears were left to moisten them . . . and over their heads, the old eaves. In one of them ivy, scarcely seen, in another, a wide walkway, worn by pigeons.

No evil omen anywhere in sight and, once more,

Out of all that longing, the lassitude, the goals and disappointments and sins, the lack and surfeit of things, the pleasures and pains,

Tender vines and foliage sprouted one day, thistles, sage, and chry-santhemums in autumn. And probably even some Rose of Sharon.

Another Folk Painting

Raki, oregano, and garlic smell strong in the pale light, that light which perforates the shutters, and the branches of the mulberry tree in the garden.

Yet it is not light. It is but the memory of brightness and thus, comes cold; winter descends, piercing hearts.

And the mulberry tree is shaken to the quick for, season after season, has it been losing its once-proud rustle.

On the Roof and Fences

A whiff of alfalfa rose with the dampness from the fields, yet the icy hoarfrost idly coated the windowpanes.

All life was in the gloom, on the roof and fences, as if some strug-gling soul, black smoke, were grasping for the heavens.

Dusk then spread over the plains and hills, but on the papers the candle wax hardened in vain.

This was, and yet was not, the landscape I longed for; something in its depths was missing, but how could I retrieve it?

Very soon, all of a sudden, the window darkened, and a dream ap-proached, luring me to sleep.

Elegy

Memory will weave that black headscarf of yours, Grandmother, as the cold north wind crochets endless skeins of yarn over the freezing village.

You wake early with a coffeepot in your hand while, in the ashes, coals still glowing plead in the hearth for evening,

With those little steps which childhood left incised in my eyes, with wrinkles which each night deepened.

Oh, autumn has fled down the hurtling torrent, and your rheumatism is always the herald of winter.

ERVIN HATIBI
1974–

Ervin Hatibi was born in Tirana and studied French at the Faculty of Foreign Language there. He managed to publish a first volume of poetry during the dictatorship, but it was during the 1990s that his unconventional verse became popular, in particular with students in Tirana and elsewhere.

His collections of verse include *I Watch the Sky Every Day* (*Përditë shoh qiellin* [Tirana, 1989]), *Poetry* (*Poezi* [Tirana, 1995]), and *Table of Contents* (*Pasqyra e lëndës* [Tirana, 2004]). He is also the author of a notable collection of essays, *Republick of Albanania* (Tirana, 2005). Hatibi is also a figurative artist who has exhibited his works both in Albania and abroad.

They'll Invent a Substance or a Machine

Soon they'll invent a substance
Or a machine, who knows, women will succeed,

And men will, too,
In slimming magically, "butterflies of some tragic drink
That go blind in the chalice of youth,"
In losing weight, their exact dimensions will scorn us.
The sweat of the architect-physician will drip, like a compass,
On that boiled rose,
That bourgeois French revolution
Which divides the bum from the back—the panting of the girl
Whom I loved for eleven years.
In short, the erotic erosion of fat will appear in the headlines.
The tests, the reactions,
Extremely precise, no trauma, the slimming machines
In clinics will exorcize all that fellow's culinary excesses,
His belly filled with savings for a subscription or a yoga course,
And the lady, sighing, will melt her rigid breasts
And will yet return with regret to the machine,
Perhaps to put on or to lose a few more pounds,
At the same time, she will firm the calves of her weary legs.
The world will be filled with the delicate creations of Rodin,
Which do it quickly, their copulating cocks like the talons of
     sparrows
On the high-voltage wires.
Then, they say that other machines will be invented,
That other substances which, buried in bright-colored phials
From the slimming labs,
Will carry off the daily
Surplus
Of fat,
Cart it down to the Third World,
To the Somalis with ribs protruding from deep beneath the earth,
And inject it into their black skins, to the arid beating of drums
Under the palm trees,
All the bums and thighs and protein-filled throats,
Bequeathed on boring Swedish afternoons in Europe,
And thus all races will become brothers and equals
And all men will be happy tattoos.

Dedicated

It looks like they're all turning around
To stare at me as I live
And feel and blush.
I know
I reek of olives,
They are stars,
Scribbled vertically
In a parish roster,
Sewn into my lungs
With the threads I once bit off
My grandmother's black scarf
(in which I often found her gray hairs).
On wretched nights I extract them, thorns
From my ankles, these Gothic olives, these daytime stars.
With them I adorn my room,
The commonplace Christmas trees
Of my lonely existence.
I also like to write poems.

Especially in August

At the beach: the sea!
Since we did not have a revolution,
Let's swim full of anger, deeper and deeper,
The farther from land, the closer to heaven,
Seagulls paid on postcards, estranged from us,
Remain
On our backs,
Or rarely even unpaid remain,
Especially now in August,
We are all a deeply tanned people,
Made of native colonists,
Half-nude, wrapped in rags of portentous colors,
We run down the beach, buying up baubles and watches,

ERVIN HATIBI

We flirt and do crazy things,
Then in the shade we pray prostrate to the sun
And baptize ourselves in the fecal seawater
(the hairy feces of women like dark-colored crabs,
Millipede priests, bind us to these pagan rites).
Day after day come trains and wagons filled with young
Internees.
Those who wanted to have a Revolution
Or make some grimace in public,
Beaten by the traffic police all year round,
Their journey ends at the sea.
Here they are brought to chill out, correct their ways
(a calming full of ardor, full of shouting thighs, motor boots
Of pumice, icy like quotations),
Only the sand is limp, wears you down, reminds us
Of the expulsion
From our homes
Or from the promised land,
But we chose the beach ourselves,
Jews disrobed, in underwear
Under a crematorium sun
Which capital freed from the ozone chains,
We rape one another reciprocally for nothing
As soon as we remove our textile masks, which as I said,
Enclose other humanities beneath.
As soon as summer comes,
The temperatures rise,
Democracy will reign over the abandoned city
Under the weary coups d'état of tourism.

Once Again on the Price of Bananas

Bananas from Rome once grew menacingly
Behind the Berlin Wall,
In the year nineteen eighty something,
Jungles of concrete and steel and panic,

Men were wolves or monks for one another, surrounded
By bananas
On an island encircled
By sparkling red water,
Ich bin ein Berliner,
But in fact, I'm an American Czech who . . .
Post-Marxism still evolutionist reproduced
Black bananas made of rubber
For post-
Stalinists, the grandsons of dervishes, to beat
Our people with (*end of quotation*),
Banana land stuffed with fried sweet potatoes,
The potato is still food, underground sustenance
Sown on the museum fields of Mauthausen, Treblinka.
With potatoes we make chips, with the other hand
In the dark we caress
The tepid belly of the television set, full of Coca-Cola,
Chips, not potatoes, are related to bananas,
Chips and bananas and the Coca-Cola, too,
All related by marriage
And dowry to Madonna,
And first gave birth to dead
Bananas from Rome
Now manufactured together
In the same clump
As black rubber cudgels.

.

■ □ ■ □ ■

SOURCE NOTES

The authors or their representatives hold the rights to the original poems. The translators have consulted the following publications of the poems while creating their translations. Original Albanian titles of the poems are listed in parentheses following their English counterparts, along with the page numbers for the consulted source.

Flutura Açka, *Festë me ankthin* (Elbasan: Onufri, 1997): "Ballad on a Campaign to Inhibit Feelings" ("Baladë fushatës së frenimit të ndjenjave," p. 47); "Monotony" ("Monotoni," p. 45); "On Our 'Ancestral Lands'" ("Në 'trojet' tona," p. 26); "Prayer for Anna Akhmatova" ("Lutje Ana Ahmatovës," p. 31).

———, *Kurth' i diellit* (Tirana: Skanderbeg Books, 2003): "Evil Doings" ("Prapësitë," p. 71).

———, *Mure vetmie* (Elbasan: Onufri, 1995): "Landscape" ("Peizazh," p. 17).

Dritëro Agolli, *Fjala gdhend gurin* (Tirana: Naim Frashëri, 1977): "The Cow" ("Lopa," p. 68).

———, *Udhëtoj i menduar* (Tirana: Naim Frashëri, 1985): "On the Appeal of Poetry" ("Për shqetësimin poetik," p. 67); "The Moon over the Meadow" ("Hëna mbi livadh," p. 141); "The Snow" ("Dëbora," p. 19); "The Wind" ("Era," p. 126).

———, *Vjen njeriu i çuditshëm* (Tirana: Dritëro, 1996): "Simple but Useful Things" ("Gjëra të thjeshta, por të dobishme," p. 15); "The Secrets of the Candle" ("Fshehtësitë e qiririt," p. 97).

Mimoza Ahmeti, *Delirium* (Tirana: Marin Barleti, 1994): "Death" ("Vdekja," p. 124); "Delirium" ("Delirium," p. 16); "Eastern Europe" ("Europë lindore," p. 19); "I'm Just Mad About Campari" ("Jam i çmendur për Kampari," p. 28); "Letter to Mommy" ("Letër mamkës,"

p. 68); "Mental Asylum with Open Doors" ("Çmendina me portë hapur," p. 12).

Fatos Arapi, *Duke dalë prej ëndrrës* (Tirana: Naim Frashëri, 1989): "I Dislike Achilles" ("Unë nuk e dua Akilin . . . ," p. 57); "Poems on My Mother" ("Për nënën time," pp. 17–19).

———, *Eklipsi i ëndrres* (Tirana: Toena, 2002): "Leaving Vlora" ("Duke u larguar prej Vlore," p. 25).

———, *Ku shkoni ju, statuja: Poezi* (Tirana: Naim Frashëri, 1990): "The Brothers of Pegasus" ("Vëllezërit e Pegasit," p. 47).

———, *Më vjen keq për Jagon* (Tirana: Albin, 1994): "Where to Inter You?" ("Ku të varros," p. 6).

———, *Ne, pikëllimi i dritave* (Tirana: Lidhja e Shkrimtarëve, 1993): "And She Turned Up" ("Dhe ajo erdhi," p. 49); "How Can I Endure the Autumn?" ("Si mund ta duroj vjeshtën," p. 59); "I Arose" ("U ngrita," p. 68); "I Awaited the Nights, Standing" ("I kam pritur netët në këmbë," p. 47); "Those Who Still Love" ("Ata që dashurojnë akoma," p. 56); "Where Is That Old Man?" ("Ku është ai plak," p. 30).

———, *Poema dhe vjersha* (Tirana: Naim Frashëri, 1966): "You Will Come" ("Ti do vish," p. 18).

Lindita Arapi, *Ndodhi në shpirt* (Elbasan: Onufri, 1985): "Bloodstain" ("Njollë gjaku," p. 49); "Energies of Color" ("Energji të ngjyrës," p. 61); "Girls Are Made of Water" ("Vajzat janë prej uji," p. 33); "Walls" ("Muret," p. 67).

Asdreni, *Psallme murgu* (Bucharest, Romania: n.p., 1930): "Forgotten Memories" ("Kujtime të shkuara," n.p.); "The Flute" ("Fyelli," n.p.); "The Oracle of Dodona" ("Fjala e Dodonës," n.p.); "To the Adriatic" ("Adriatikut," n.p.).

Eqrem Basha, *Udha qumështore* (Prishtina, Kosova: Rilindja, 1986): "Cold" ("Ftohtë," p. 37); "Nighttime Traveler of This World" ("Udhëtar i natës së kësaj bote," p. 15).

———, *Zogu i zi* (Skopje, Macedonia: Flaka e Vëllazërimit, 1995): "Balkan Menu" ("Meny ballkanik," p. 31); "The Audience" ("Audienca," p. 132); "The Nightingale Sings" ("Këndon bilbili," p. 93); "The Street Sweepers of Prishtina" ("Larësit e Prishtinës," p. 32); "The Wolf" ("Ujku," p. 89).

Mario Bellizzi, *Last Exit to Bukura Morea* (Castrovillari, Italy: Il Coscile, 2003): "Aroma" ("Erë e mirë," p. 32); "Curfew" ("Orë policore," p. 76); "Serbs, Coca-Cola, and Kosovars" ("Serbë—Coca-Cola & Kosovarë," p. 98); "Trance" ("Trance," p. 98).

Bernardin Palaj and Donat Kurti, eds., *Visaret e kombit*, vol. 2 (Tirana: Nikaj, 1937): "Gjergj Elez Alia" ("Gjergj Elez Alia," pp. 42–48;

recorded in Nikaj [district of Tropoja]); "Omer, Son of Mujo" ("Omer prej Mujit," pp. 203–10; oral version composed by Mëhill Prêka); "The Marriage of Gjeto Basho Mujo" ("Gjeto Basho Muji: Martesa," pp. 1–10; oral version composed by Mëhill Prêka); "The Source of Mujo's Strength" ("Fuqija e Mujit," pp. 63–66; oral version composed by Mëhill Prêka).

Pjetër Bogdani, *Cuneus prophetarum* (Padua, Italy: Typographia Seminarii, 1685): "The Cumaean Sibyl" ("Sibila Cumea," p. 161); "The Cumanian Sibyl" ("Sibila Cumana," p. 170); "The Delphic Sibyl" ("Sibila Delfica," p. 164); "The Erythraean Sibyl" ("Sibila Eritrea," pp. 166–68); "The Hellespontic Sibyl" ("Sibila Elespontica," p. 172); "The Libyan Sibyl" ("Sibila Libica," pp. 162–63); "The Persian Sibyl" ("Sibila Persica," p. 165); "The Phrygian Sibyl" ("Sibila Frigia," p. 173); "The Samian Sibyl" ("Sibila Samia," p. 169); "The Tiburtine Sibyl" ("Sibila Tiburtina," p. 175).

Andon Zako Çajupi, *Baba-Tomorri* (Cairo, Egypt: n.p., 1902): "Motherland" ("Mëmëdheu," n.p.); "My Village" ("Fshati im," n.p.); "Servitude" ("Robëria," n.p.).

Martin Camaj, *Lirika midis dy moteve* (Munich, Germany: n.p., 1967): "First Elegy" ("Elegjí e parë," p. 13); "Mountain Feast" ("Drekë malsore," p. 48).

———, *Njeriu më vete e me tjerë* (Munich, Germany: n.p., 1978): "A Bird Languishes" ("Një zog lëngon," p. 8); "Abandoned Village" ("Katund i lanun mbas dore," p. 62); "Avalanche" ("Mal i rrëxuem," p. 17); "Death—Crackling" ("Vdekje—Krizëm," p. 14); "Disregard" ("Mospërfillje," p. 11); "Failure" ("Deshtimi," p. 27); "Fragile Land" ("Vend i thyeshëm," p. 87); "Fragment" ("Fragment," p. 41); "Hostile Sea" ("Deti anmik," p. 72); "My Mother" ("Ime amë," p. 21); "That Mountain of Ice Divides Time" ("Ai mal akulli ndan kohën," p. 40); "There Before the Tribes Arrived" ("Aty si tash para se me ardhë fiset," p. 31); "In the Shade of Things" ("Në hijen e sendeve," p. 33); "To a Modern Poet" ("Nji poeti të sotëm," p. 37); "Two Generations" ("Dy brezni," p. 53); "Unexpected Guest in Berisha" ("Mysafir i papritun në Berishë," p. 15); "Winter" ("Dimën," p. 21).

Basri Çapriqi, *Frutat bizare* (Prishtina, Kosova: Rilindja, 1996): "Girl from the East, Prostitute in Rome" ("Vasha nga lindja prostitutë në Romë," p. 37); "My Room in London" ("Dhoma ime në Londër," p. 12); "My Room in Ulqin" ("Dhoma ime në Ulqin," p. 23).

Romeo Çollaku, *Kumbaraja e kohës* (Tirana: Ombra GVG, 2004): "Another Folk Painting" ("Tjetër pikturë popullore," p. 18); "Elegy" ("Elegji," p. 25); "Lost in Thought" ("Mendueshëm," p. 8); "Old Faded

Photographs" ("Fotografi të vjetra, të zverdhura," p. 12); "On the Roof and Fences" ("Mbi çati e gjerdhe," p. 20); "Song of the Horned Lark" ("Kënga e çerdhuklës," p. 9); "The Piggy Bank of Time" ("Kumbaraja e kohës," p. 7).

Girolamo De Rada, *Canti di Milosao* (Naples, Italy: Guttenberg, 1836): "Can a Kiss Be Sweeter?" (excerpt from *Canti di Milosao,* canto 4); "Like Two Radiant Lips" (excerpt from *Canti di Milosao,* canto 2); "The Earth Had Transformed the Oaks" (excerpt from *Canti di Milosao,* canto 1).

Gjergj Fishta, *The Highland Lute: The Albanian National Epic,* trans. Robert Elsie and Janice Mathie-Heck (London: Centre for Albanian Studies, 2005): "Bec Patani Meets His Blood Brother in Battle" (excerpt from *Lahuta e malcís,* canto 20, lines 581–616, 696–768, 783–817); "Mehmet Ali Pasha" (excerpt from *Lahuta e malcís,* canto 10, lines 1–400); "The Mountain Nymphs Mourn the Death of Tringa" (excerpt from *Lahuta e malcís,* canto 24, lines 662–787).

Italo Costante Fortino, ed., *Giulio Variboba: La vita di Maria* (Cosenza, Italy: Brenner, 1984): "The Life of the Virgin Mary" (excerpt from *Ghiella e Shën Mëriis Virghiër,* pp. 68–71); "The Song of the Awakening" (excerpt from "Kenka e të zgjuarit," pp. 106–10).

Naim Frashëri, *Bagëti e bujqësija* (Bucharest, Romania: Dritë, 1886): "O Mountains of Albania" (excerpt from "O malet' e Shqipërisë," n.p.).

———, *Luletë e verësë* (Bucharest, Romania: Dituri, 1890): "The Flute" ("Fyelli," n.p.).

———, *Vjersha për mësonjëtoret të para* (Bucharest, Romania: Dritë, 1886): "The Words of the Candle" ("Fjalët' e qiririt," n.p.).

Sabri Hamiti, *Leja e njohtimit* (Prishtina, Kosova: Rilindja, 1985): "George Castrioti" ("Gjergj Castrioti," p. 13).

———, *Trungu ilir* (Prishtina, Kosova: Rilindja, 1983): "Ali Podrimja" ("Ali Podrimja," p. 321); "Prizren" ("Prizren," p. 306); "The Telegram" ("Telegrami," p. 278); "The Telephone" ("Telefoni," p. 291).

Mihal Hanxhari, *Gdhend një statujë* (Tirana: Toena, 2005): "A Severed Prayer" ("Lutja e këputur," p. 17); "Leaves" ("Gjethe," p. 21); "Lemon Blossoms" ("Lule limoni," p. 190); "Night of Stillness" ("Natë heshtje," p. 16); "Petals" ("Petale," p. 20); "Rapture" ("Dehje," p. 186); "The Cypress Trees" ("Qiparisat," p. 36); "The Earth" ("Toka," p. 32); "The Linden Trees" ("Bliret," p. 28); "The Storm" ("Stuhiu," p. 33); "To Sleep" ("Në gjumë," p. 42); "Unquenchable Fire" ("Zjarr që s'shuhet," p. 187); "Voiceless" ("Pa zë," p. 41); "Where Is" ("Ku është," p. 195); "While on Its Way" ("Gjersa erdhi," p. 40); "Without You" ("Pa ty," p. 43).

Ervin Hatibi, *Pasqyra e lëndës* (Tirana: Ora, 2004): "Once Again on the Price of Bananas" ("Edhe një herë mbi çmimin e bananeve," p. 37).

———, *Poezi* (Tirana: Marin Barleti, 1995): "Dedicated" ("Kushtuar," p. 51); "Especially in August" ("Sidomos në gusht," p. 58); "They'll Invent a Substance or a Machine" ("Do të shpiket një lëngë ose makinë," pp. 40–41).

Mahmud Hysa, ed., *Autorë dhe tekste nga letërsia e vjetër shqiptare*, vol. 2 (Skopje, Macedonia: Flaka e Vëllazërimit, 1995): "Lord, Don't Leave Me Without Coffee" ("Imzot, mos më lerë pa kahve," pp. 114–15); "Money" (excerpt from "Paraja," pp. 156–60); "Trahaná" ("Trahani," pp. 164–65).

Rexhep Ismajli, ed., *Pjetër Budi: Poezi (1618–1621)* (Prishtina, Kosova: Rilindja, 1986): "O Hapless, Luckless Man" (excerpt from "O paa fati nierij," pp. 64–67); "The Deed of Cain" (excerpt from "Si muorë me u nçtuom," pp. 114–15).

Abdullah Konushevci, *Pikat AD* (Prishtina, Kosova: Rilindja, 2002): "Dream . . . Then Vlora" ("Ëndrra . . . pastaj Vlora," p. 20); "Expressionist Verse" ("Vjershë ekspresioniste," p. 25); "Heavy Burden, Your Fragile Body" ("Barrë e madhe, trupi yt i thyeshëm," p. 78); "How Prishtina Once Woke in the Morning" ("Si zgjohej Prishtina në mëngjes," p. 31); "The Honorable Whore" ("Lavirja e denjë," p. 32).

Mitrush Kuteli, *Sulm e lotë* (Tirana: Nikaj, 1944): "The Muddy Albanian Soil" ("Balta shqipëtare," pp. 55–57).

Arian Leka, *Strabizëm* (Tetova, Macedonia: Ditët e Naimit, 2004): "Alone" ("Vetëm," p. 12); "Background Chant" ("Kabá," p. 35); "Easter on the Island of Hvar" ("Pashka në ishullin Hvar," p. 31); "The Spine of the Sea" ("Shpina e detit," p. 9).

Leka (Shkodra) 10 (1937): "Freedom" ("Lirija," n.p.).

Luljeta Lleshanaku, *Antipastorale* (Tirana: Eurorilindja, 1999): "Always a Premonition" ("Gjithmonë një parandjenjë," p. 75); "Annual Snowfall" ("Dëbora e përvitshme," p. 13); "Chamomile Breath" ("Frymë kamomili," pp. 58–59); "Mutual Understanding" ("Mirëkuptim," p. 45).

———, *Palca e verdhë* (Prishtina, Kosova: Gjon Buzuku, 2000): "Electrolysis" ("Elektroliza," p. 106); "For as Long As" ("Për sa kohë," p. 109); "Quite by Accident" ("Krejt rastësisht," p. 100); "The Old People's Home" ("Azili," p. 68); "The Truth" ("E vërteta," p. 130).

———, *Preludë poetike* (Tirana: Naim Frashëri, 1990): "With You" ("Me ty," n.p.).

Sejfullah Malëshova, *Vjersha* (Tirana: n.p., 1945): "How I Love Albania" ("Si e dua Shqipërinë," pp. 18–19); "Rebel Poet" ("Poeti rebel," pp. 13–16).

SOURCE NOTES

Manuscripts, Fondi 43, D2, D3, D4 in the Albanian National Archives, Tirana, Albania: "Friends of Mine, They Are Fine Fellows" ("Disa miq, disa jaranë," ca. 1735); "I'm Your Slave, You Are My Love" ("Më ke rop e të kam xhan," ca. 1735); "In the Dust Left by Your Footsteps" ("Degù ej mal u maksud," ca. 1735); "Nezim Has Made It Merry" ("Divan kush pat folturë shqip?" ca. 1735); "Oh, Your Gaze, That Slicing Saber" ("Ej gamzen shemshir i burran," ca. 1735); "Some Young Fellows Have Now Turned Up" ("Duallë ca nev zuhurë," ca. 1735); "We Have Set Off into Exile" ("Jemi nisurë në gurbet," ca. 1735).

Lekë Matrënga, *Embsuame e chraesterae* (Rome, Italy: Guglielmo Facciotto, 1592): "Spiritual Song" ("Cghíthaeue u thaerés . . . ," n.p.).

Din Mehmeti, *Antologjia personale* (Tirana: Ora, 2004): "I Have One Request" ("Kam një porosi," p. 121); "My Sailboat" ("Varka ime," p. 114); "Self-Portrait" ("Autoportret," p. 13); "The Past" ("E kaluar," p. 119).

————, *Klithmë është emri im* (Tirana: Toena, 2002): "A Legend" ("Një legjendë," p. 141); "Night of the Poets" ("Nata e poetëve," p. 81); "Swollen Roads" ("Rrugët e fryra," p. 209).

Esad Mekuli, *Brigjet* (Prishtina, Kosova: Rilindja, 1981): "Evening" ("Mbramja," p. 11); "Hope" ("Shpresa," p. 136); "I" ("Unë," p. 28); "Is It the Albanian's Fault?" ("A asht fajtor shqiptari," p. 44); "The Death of Day" ("Vdekja e ditës," p. 17).

Migjeni, *Vargjet e lira* (Tirana: Ismail Mal' Osmani, 1944): "Autumn on Parade" ("Vjeshta në parakalim," p. 41); "Blasphemy" ("Blasfemi," p. 26); "Fragment" ("Fragment," p. 46); "Poem of Poverty" ("Poema e mjerimit," pp. 19–23); "Resignation" ("Rezignata," p. 45); "Scandalous Song" ("Kanga skandaloze," p. 43); "Song of Noble Grief" ("Kanga e dhimbës krenare," p. 35); "Suffering" ("Vuejtja," pp. 85–86); "The Themes" ("Motivet," pp. 49–59); "Under the Banners of Melancholy" ("Nën flamujt e melankolisë," pp. 90–91).

Ndre Mjeda, *Juvenilia* (Vienna, Austria: Vernay, 1917): "Winter" ("Dimni," n.p.).

————, *Vepra letrare*, vol. 1 (Tirana: Naim Frashëri, 1988): "To the Albanian Eagle" ("Shqypes arbnore," pp. 157–60).

Besnik Mustafaj, *Legjenda e lindjes sime* (Tirana: Ora, 2005): "Donika" ("Donika," pp. 63–64); "I've Set Off to Find You" ("Jam nisure të të mbërrij," p. 111); "Night Walk in the Forest" ("Shëtitje natën në pyll," p. 71); "Prophetic Poem" ("Poemë profetike," p. 98); "The Heroes and I" ("Unë dhe heronjtë," p. 20); "Whence Your Fear of the Wolf" ("Nga të vjen kjo frikë prej ujkut," p. 112).

Fan Noli, *Albumi* (Boston: Vatra, 1948): "Dead in Exile" ("Syrgjyn-vdekur," n.p.); "On Riverbanks" ("Anës lumenjve," n.p.); "Run, O Soldier of Marathon" ("Rent or Marathonomak," n.p.).

Arshi Pipa, *Libri i burgut* (Rome, Italy: Apice, 1959): "Dawn" ("Agim," p. 28); "The Canal" ("Kanali," p. 63); "The First Night" ("Natë e parë," p. 27); "The Lamp" ("Llampa," p. 28).

Ali Podrimja, *Buzëqeshja në kafaz* (Klagenfurt, Austria: Wieser, 1993): "Or Rather" ("Ose, ose," p. 32); "The Albanians" ("Shqiptarët," p. 16).

———, *Folja* (Prishtina, Kosova: Rilindja, 1973): "The Illness of My Family" ("Sëmundja e familjes sime," n.p.).

———, *Fund i gëzuar* (Prishtina, Kosova: Rilindja, 1988): "If" ("Nëse," p. 64); "It Is the Albanian's Fault" ("Fajtor është shqiptari," pp. 62–63); "The Meadow" ("Livadhi," p. 46).

———, *Lum Lumi* (Prishtina, Kosova: Rilindja, 1982): "And You Dead" ("E ti i vdekur," p. 70); "Death Was Quicker" ("Vdekja ishte më e shpejtë," p. 72); "The Dead Clock" ("Ora e vdekur," p. 7).

———, *Sampo* (Prishtina, Kosova: Rilindja, 1969): "Ghazal" ("Gazela," n.p.).

———, *Zari* (Prishtina, Kosova: Rilindja, 1990): "A Child Is Dying in the Cellar" ("Fëmija vdes në bodrum," p. 33); "Who Will Slay the Wolf" ("Kush do ta vrasë ujkun," p. 16).

Lasgush Poradeci, *Vdekja e nositit* (Prishtina, Kosova: Rilindja, 1986): "End of Autumn" ("Mbarim vjeshte," p. 83); "Morning" ("Mëngjes," p. 81); "Pogradec" ("Poradeci," p. 67); "Winter" ("Dimër," p. 84).

Giuseppe Serembe, *Vjershe* (Milan, Italy: Grandi Editore, 1926): "Friendship" ("Mikjëria," n.p.); "Song of Longing" ("Kënthimë tharosi," n.p.).

Azem Shkreli, *E di një fjalë prej guri* (Prishtina, Kosova: Rilindja, 1969): "Before the Elegy" ("Para elegjisë," n.p.); "With Migjeni" ("Me Migjenin," n.p.).

———, *Kënga e hutinit* (Prishtina, Kosova: Rilindja, 1986): "A Tale About Us" ("Rrëfimi për ne," p. 34); "Anathema" ("Anatema," p. 51); "Frightened Light" ("Dritë e trembur," p. 47); "Monument to Mic Sokoli" ("Përmendore për M. Sokoli," p. 19); "Obituary for a Bird" ("Nekrolog për zogun," p. 7); "The Toast" ("Dollia," p. 38).

———, *Lirikë me shi* (Prishtina, Kosova: Lumi, 1994): "Departure of the Migrants" ("Nisja e mërgimtarëve," p. 20); "Martin's Stone" ("Guri i Martinit," p. 99).

———, *Nata e papagajve* (Prishtina, Kosova: Rilindja, 1990): "Wolf's Spoor" ("Gjurmë ujku," p. 44).

SOURCE NOTES

————, *Nga Bibla e heshtjes* (Prishtina, Kosova: Rilindja, 1975): "Over Europe" ("Mbi Evropë," n.p.); "The Death of the Highlander" ("Vdekja e malsorit," n.p.).

————, *Zogj dhe gurë* (Prishtina, Kosova: Gazeta Rilindja, 1997): "Song of Shame" ("Këngë e turpshme," p. 118).

Xhevahir Spahiu, *Ferrparajsa* (Elbasan: Onufri, 1994): "Kosova" ("Kosova," p. 64).

————, *Heshtje s'ka* (Tirana: Naim Frashëri, 1989): "In the Roots of Words" ("Tek rrënja e fjalëve," pp. 29–30).

————, *Kohë e krisur* (Tirana: Lidhja e Shkrimtarëve, 1991): "Our History" ("Historia jonë," p. 105); "Sketch" ("Vizatim," p. 70); "Speech" ("Fjala," pp. 11–12); "To Wake Up Late" ("Të zgjohesh vonë," p. 21); "Translation of the River" ("Përkthimi i lumit," p. 71).

————, *Rreziku* (Tirana: Ideart, 2003): "Torquemada" ("Torquemada," p. 71).

————, *Vdekje perëndive* (Tirana: Naim Frashëri, 1977): "To Be with You" ("Të jesh me ty," p. 75).

Parid Teferiçi, *Meqenëse sytë* (Tirana: Aleph, 2003): "First Prayer" ("Lutja e parë," p. 67); "In a Country as Small as This One" ("Në një vend të vogël si ky," p. 76); "In Obot, While Waiting" ("Në Obot, duke pritur," p. 20); "In Perspective" ("Në perspektivë," pp. 42–43); "The Poet" ("Poeti," p. 50); *"Woman Holding a Balance*, by Vermeer" ("*Peshuesja e perlave*, Vermeer," p. 44).

Kasëm Trebeshina, *Lirika dhe satira* (Tirana: Marin Barleti, 1994): "Evening" ("Mbrëmje," p. 80); "The Iceberg" ("Aisbergu," p. 3); "The Pelicans" ("Pelikanët," p. 67); "The Storks" ("Lejlekët," pp. 65–66); "We Met in the Darkness" ("U njohëm në errësirë," p. 5).

Agron Tufa, *Rrethinat e Atlantidës* (Tirana: Aleph, 2002): "Albania" ("Shqipëria," p. 49); "Old Stanza for a New Love" ("Stancë e vjetër për dashurinë e re," p. 15); "The Proof of the Land" ("Prova e tokës," p. 71); "The Regulations at the Catholic School for Girls" ("Rregullat e Shkollës Katolike të Vajzave," pp. 69–70).

Pashko Vasa, *Vepra*, vol. 1 (Prishtina, Kosova: Rilindja, 1989): "O Albania, Poor Albania" ("O moj Shqypni," pp. 73–77).

Yll Zajmi, ed., *Antologji e letërsisë së vjetër shqipe* (Prishtina, Kosova: Enti i Teksteve, 1985): "I Traveled the Earth" ("Po rraha dhera," p. 144); "Of Honorable Lineage" ("Farie së ndeerme në Kuntisë u bii," pp. 143–44).

Visar Zhiti, *Dyert e gjalla* (Tirana: Eurorilindja, 1995): "In Our Cells" ("Në qeli," p. 22); "The Tyrant's Onetime Office, Near Which I Work" ("Zyra e dikurshme e diktatorit, pranë së cilës punoj," p. 95).

————, *Hedh një kafkë* (Tirana: Naim Frashëri, 1994): "Death Impresses No One Here" ("Vdekja këtu nuk trondit kërkënd," p. 116); "Little Prison, Big Prison" ("Burgu i vogël, burgu i madh," p. 70); "The Prison Shower Room" ("Banjoja e të burgosurve," pp. 134–35).

————, *Kujtesa e ajrit* (Tirana: Lidhja e Shkrimtarëve, 1993): "At the Bars of My Cell" ("Te hekurat e frengjisë sime," p. 68).

————, *Mbjellja e vetëtimave* (Skopje, Macedonia: Flaka e vëllazërimit, 1994): "Bloody Lips" ("Buzët mbi gjak," p. 31).

————, *Si shkohet në Kosovë* (Tirana: Toena, 2000): "Far from Our Countries" ("Larg vendeve tona," p. 35); "My Father's Poem" ("Poema e babait," pp. 22–23).

Zef Zorba, *Buzë të ngrira në gaz* (Tirana: Dituria, 1994): "A Moment, Poetry: Life" ("Një çast, poezi: Një jetë," p. 8); "A Nail" ("Një gozdhë," p. 78); "Feast Tonight" ("Sonte festë," p. 20); "Kruja" ("Kruja," p. 28); "Like Swallows" ("Si zogjë dallëndysheje," p. 21); "Roads in Autumn" ("Rrugët në vjeshtë," p. 43); "Somber This Path" ("I errët ky shteg," p. 6); "The Gravel of the Kir" ("Zalli i Kirit," p. 23); "Yearning" ("Malle," p. 11).

■ □ ■ □ ■

WRITINGS FROM AN UNBOUND EUROPE

For a complete list of titles, see the Writings from an Unbound Europe Web site at www.nupress.northwestern.edu/ue.